MAKING LOVE ON SCRABBLE

By

Dr. Karen Hutchins Pirnot

DPB

Copyright 2015 by Dr. Karen Hutchins Pirnot

All rights reserved

For information regarding permission, contact:

www.drpirnotbooks.com

ISBN 13: 978-1517759148

ISBN 10: 1517759145

Printed in the United States of America

Printed: January 2016

Dr. Pirnot Books via Create Space

FOREWORD

In my first book about being an Alzheimer's caregiver (**NOTHING LEFT TO BURN**), I talked about my own thoughts, feelings and behaviors while transitioning through the stages of the disease with my husband Charlie (a composite character based on many of the dementia patients I have assessed and treated over the years). The focus of that book was on the caregiver and how we can be sucked into the disease and lose out on life if we fail to engage in "due diligence" for ourselves. In this book, I wanted to focus on one of the most important aspects of dementia patients, that being daily emotional well-being.

Because of the insidious nature of the disease, we caregivers oftentimes get caught up in our fears, frustrations and anger such that we fail to take advantage of easy opportunities to actually assist those in our care through difficult emotional times. In this book, I am focusing on those small, seemingly frustrating moments when instead of sighing and letting out a breath of exasperation, we can actually reframe what we have just experienced into something positive for the dementia patients in our care.

Sometimes, if we will but take a deep breath and think about a frustrating situation, we can actually see the humor of it. We can then reframe it for the dementia patient such that s/he will begin to feel a sense of momentary worth. Granted, it will not carry over to another such incident, but we actually have dozens of opportunities daily to reverse a difficult situation. We can oftentimes avoid putting loved ones on medications for anxiety or depression if we can keep their morale boosted until the final stages of the disease.

It is with this thought in mind that I have written **MAKING LOVE ON SCRABBLE.** The incidents are real and when I look back on them, I realize that my own mental health took a turn for the positive when I began to reframe the anger and frustration I felt for the hideous disease afflicting my husband. Hopefully, it will be of some help to you as well.

Dr. Karen Hutchins Pirnot

Dedicated to all those who struggle with brain disease – and most especially, to those who care for them.

1.

Principles of Reinforcement

Relative to Those With Dementia

The ideas of positive reinforcement are time-honored principles, based on substantial research by researchers (Pavlov, Skinner, Thorndike, and Watson) in psychology, learning theory and behaviorism. The principles of positive reinforcement do not use any type of negative feedback (yelling, humiliation, pain, guilt, intimidation or shame) to encourage appropriate behavior.

Positive reinforcement is intended to modify troublesome behaviors and/or encourage more appropriate behaviors. It is generally used in child behavioral modification but is also useful in geriatric settings in which disease symptoms or environmental factors produce confusion, anxiety and/or depression which leads to maladaptive behavior on the part of the patient.

Anxiety and depression are common features in Alzheimer's disease as well as in other progressive dementias such as Parkinson's disease, Lewy body disease, vascular dementia and frontal-temporal dementia. Particularly during the moderate to severe stages of the disease, it is important to keep patients feeling calm and secure. As their immediate world becomes increasingly more unknowable and foreign, the ability to maintain a positive and balanced emotional state is helpful both to the patient and to the caregiver(s).

While working with patients in skilled nursing facilities, it quickly became apparent that if the patient was able to maintain positive feelings about his or her care team, that patient was much more likely to function more adaptively regarding activities of daily living. Those with belligerent or angry feelings oftentimes appeared more disorganized and unable to find their way out of the quagmire of negative emotions.

As a caregiver, you don't need to memorize complicated terms or study extensively in order to effectively create an atmosphere of positive reinforcement. Here are a few common terms to remember:

Reinforcers: This is anything that motivates the patient to comply with requests for compliance or appropriate behavior. Some reinforcers may be social in nature such as a smile, an "attaboy" (saying something like "great job" or "I like what you're doing") or engaging in a social activity with a caregiver or someone else who understands the limitations of the dementia patient. Other reinforcers might be to watch a certain television show, go on a ride, listen to pleasing music, or have a treat which is acceptable to the caregiver. You simply need to know what brings momentary pleasure to your loved one, and that is probably a potential reinforcer.

Schedules of Reinforcement: When and how often to reinforce children is based upon many circumstances. When dealing with Alzheimer's and other progressive dementias, it is best to adopt a program of continual reinforcement. This means that every time your loved one does something appropriate or something which might deserve encouragement, the caregiver will reinforce immediately.

7

Those with progressive dementia do **not** remember previous efforts to reinforce their behavior. But I strongly believe that the **feelings** of pleasure of efficacy do carry over for some time. If the reinforcement is ongoing and fairly frequent, then a feeling of general well-being has a strong probability of carrying on from one moment to the next. It stands to reason that the same would be true of negative reinforcement such as shouting or angry feedback of frustration from the caregiver. My contention is that it is just as easy to give positive reinforcement as it is to negatively reinforce out of frustration and impatience.

Almost every situation has the potential for positive reinforcement. If the caregiver can simply withhold negative comments and/or actions during a tense situation, there is almost always the opportunity to learn another way to give positive feedback to the patient. Although Alzheimer's patients may not show their own feelings of confusion and humiliation at their own wrongdoing, it is surely there, just underneath the facial presentation of indifference.

Effectiveness: Although effectiveness of one's efforts on behalf of those with progressive dementia is difficult to measure, lessening of anxious behaviors and perhaps decreases in the need for medication for anxiety and depression might be indications that the reinforcements of the caregiver are having an overall positive effect.

2.

Negative Versus Positive Reinforcement

The reason positive feedback is so important to those with dementia is that it reinforces the good feelings. In this case, it reinforces the emotions of safety and efficacy that will encourage the patient to cooperate with her/his caregiver. It also builds a feeling of trust. Like a child, the dementia patients want approval and they will trust those who appear to like and respect them.

Punishing verbal words and actions do not strengthen positive behaviors and emotions. If the dementia patient shies away from the caregiver after harsh words, a learning experience is lost. Anxiety takes hold and the patient then waits for an expected negative response. After a period of time, depression and/or anxiety is likely to set in as the patient loses more and more self-respect.

Extinction in dementia patients is a condition whereby the patient is not positively reinforced for an acceptable behavior and s/he soon quits displaying that behavior. If the emotion is a smile and is not reciprocated, the patient soon ceases the behavior as it brings no reinforcement. Therefore, every interaction with a dementia patient is an opportunity for encouraging a positive feeling.

Negative reinforcement is the condition whereby a negative behavior or emotion is reinforced by some sort of attention. This is probably the most difficult for the caregiver to handle. If the patient becomes belligerent or angry and starts spewing obscenities or places him/herself in harm's way due to dangerous behaviors, you cannot simply ignore the behavior. Neither do you want to give the situation a reinforcing nature such as showing open disapproval or even fear so that your own behavior then becomes the focus of attention and the negative behavior of the patient is reinforced because of its effect on you. Since the dementia patient sees no way out of a difficult situation and cannot conceptualize another response, the emotion takes over. Oftentimes, a tantrum can be ignored if the dementia patient is not in immediate danger. But it is wise for the caregiver to remain in the room to monitor the behaviors until the tantrum has subsided. At that time, nothing is mentioned about the negative behavior. The caregiver might ask if the dementia patient would care for a glass of water of juice. If accepted, the caregiver may then reinforce the quieted patient by talking and then saying something like, "I like the way you're talking with me."

It does no good to bring up the recent negative behavior as the dementia patient likely has already forgotten about it.

A word of caution: If a caregiver ever feels her/his physical person to be in danger from a dementia patient, authorities should be called and the incident documented.

I oftentimes find that a cell phone camera comes in handy to document both positive and negative incidents. The positive ones can be shown to the dementia patient to reinforce previous good behaviors while the negative ones may be documented to ascertain whether negative behaviors are increasing in frequency and/or intensity.

It is highly unlikely that you can influence negative behaviors of the dementia patient by talking and explaining infractions in social propriety or even try to explain how you feel about the negative behavior. What we are after in a positive reinforcement program is to keep the dementia patient who is in the moderate stage of his/her disease in a condition where reinforcement produces cooperation with the caregiver.

Positive caregiver statements might be something like this:

"I just love your smile."

"I like the way you showed me what you need."

"It makes me feel good when you tell me about........"

"I like the way you (dressed yourself, brushed your teeth, talked with....)

"I love your colorful socks. (Even if they don't match, the patient got them on him/herself!)

"You are taking the time to chew your food today. That's great!"

It's a good idea to vary your responses as even those with dementia will tire of hearing the same thing all the time.

3.

The Very Best Frog Catcher in the World
Opportunity for Reinforcement

Now that there is a basic understanding of the concept of reinforcing the thoughts, feelings and behaviors of dementia patients, we need to look for opportunities to reinforce. Here's a clear example of a positive behavior in a cognitively challenged dementia patient which warrants positive reinforcement from the caregiver. Again, I draw from personal experience, using my husband as a composite character.

It was dusk and I could hear the annoying squawking of yet another frog. It was a warm spring night in Florida and the frogs were in full mating behavior. I wandered outside to check for frogs and sure, enough, there was one perched high inside the storm shutters. He looked defiant, as if he could hop away at a moment's notice to find yet another homeowner to annoy. It was time to call the captain.

"Charlie," I said as I walked back into the house. "There's a frog inside the shutter just to the left of the door as you walk outside."

"Huh?"

"Charlie, there's a frog."

"Where is it?'

12

"Outside behind the shutter?"

"Which one?"

"To your right as you go outside."

Charlie left the comfort of his recliner and went to the bedroom to put on his Sebago shoes. He came back and headed to the front door, shoes on and with a decided slump in his back and a shuffling of feet on the hardwood floor.

"What am I doing? Charlie asked.

"Charlie, I heard a frog outside. I'd like you to try to remove it."

"Okay, where is it?"

"Let me walk outside with you and I'll point to it, Charlie"

"Okay."

I led Charlie out the glass storm door and closed it quietly. I knew if he went out behind me, he would allow the door to close, thus alerting the uninvited frog quest.

I gave the finger-to-the mouth signal for Charlie to be quiet as I carefully closed the screen door. Sure enough, to the right of the door, the frog was still behind the storm shutter.

I went back inside to allow Charlie to perform his magical removal trick with frogs. After about a minute, I went back to the glass door and saw Charlie with a right-hand fist and I assumed he had the frog. He took it down the street. I never asked what Charlie did with the frogs he caught because I don't want to know.

13

Charlie came back into the house and he started to shake his right hand.

"Charlie, is your hand wet?"

"Yeah, I guess."

"Charlie, did the frog pee in your hand because it was scared?"

"It wasn't scared."

"Charlie, did the frog pee in your hand?"

"Yeah, I think so."

"Charlie, please go into your bathroom. Please wash your hand, Charlie."

"Okay."

Charlie obediently went into the bathroom and I had no idea what he did in there. But, I did hear water running. I thought I had a 50-50 chance that Charlie was washing his hands.

When Charlie came out of the bathroom, I asked if he'd washed his hands and he nodded that he had, indeed, washed his hands.

"Charlie, I just don't know how you do that," I said. "Whenever I try to catch the frogs, I somehow alert them. They always hop away from me."

Charlie produced a huge grin and he then proceeded to explain. "You have to have good hands."

Charlie made a sweeping movement with his right hand, suggesting that he simply swooped up the frog in one swift motion.

"Show me again, Charlie," I requested. Charlie again made the identical sweeping movement.

"You have to know how to do it," Charlie said.

Charlie shuffled back to his comfy recliner and I sat looking at him for a moment. Then, with a smile of my own, I said, "Charlie, I think you must be the very best frog catcher in the world!"

"I am," Charlie replied in agreement.

Charlie seemed to visibly relax. On most evenings, he would begin a routine of tapping his hands and sometimes, his feet. A friend had given me a small tactile quilt. It had various fabrics that had different tactile sensations and Charlie could rub the various sections of the quilt and it would quiet his hands. On most nights, I would ask Charlie to use the quilt so his anxiety would be lessened. That night, the quilt stayed to his side and he kept the gentle grin on his face until he went to bed.

At the time of the frog incident, Charlie was several years into the insidious Alzheimer's disease which had robbed us of our retirement dreams. His adaptive functioning was very childlike and he was basically totally dependent upon me for everything except for toileting. Charlie was becoming increasingly anxious and had developed many annoying routines. I was continually searching for ways for him to become more confident about himself. And that night, I think I stumbled upon a form of affirmation that also seemed to have a calming effect.

Even though I had attempted to positively reinforce Charlie at the first signs of the disease, that night I vowed to look for other such opportunities daily. If my Charlie was the very best frog catcher in the world, he undoubtedly had other talents I had failed to recognize.

Do not dwell in the past, do not dream of the future,
*concentrate the mind on the present moment.   **Buddha***

4.

THE VERY CREATIVE INTERPRETER

Providing Reinforcement through the Fog of Dementia

I'd been out mowing our small, front yard while Charlie watched television. When I came back inside, I saw my husband staring at the screen with a puzzled look on his face.

"Charlie, what are you watching?" I asked.

"The news," my husband replied.

I looked at the television screen and then said, "Charlie you're watching a women's softball game. It's Baylor and Oklahoma and Oklahoma is up 3-2."

"Oh, is that what it is?" Charlie asked.

"Yes, that's what it is, Charlie."

"Well, they shouldn't tell me it's the news then," Charlie replied.

"Charlie, have you been watching this program the whole time while I was outside mowing the lawn?

"Yeah."

"Well, it's a softball game, Charlie. Is that what you want?"

"Yeah."

"But, it's not the news, Charlie."

"Yes it is. It's news to me."

"Well, Charlie, you want to know what I think?"

"Yeah."

"I think you are a very creative interpreter of what you see on television!"

"Thank you," Charlie said with a smile.

When there is mental confusion, it is sometimes difficult to look for an opportunity to reinforce. You oftentimes need to look beyond the obvious mental fog and look to what lies beneath the surface. In this case, Charlie was attempting a vicarious participation in a current event. Even though he was not particularly successful, it was important for him to have someone else notice his efforts in attempting to track the current environment. So, in this story, the reinforcement was for an attempt to participate. Referring to Charlie's mental abilities as "creative" rather than as "deficient" is an act of positive reinforcement which promotes a sense of emotional well-being.

Life is really simple, but we insist on making it complicated.   Confucius

5.

THE MENTAL MAGICIAN

A Case of Elusive Clues

I could hear the shower running but I stuck my head in the bedroom and saw that Charlie was dressing. The television set in his room was on.

"Charlie, would you please turn off the shower?" I asked.

Charlie went to the television set and he turned it off.

"Thank you for turning off the television, Charlie. But now, can you please turn off the shower. The water has been running a long time."

"I just turned it off."

That one stumped me for a moment until I turned the television back on and saw that it was raining in the program on the screen. It must have confused Charlie.

"Charlie, you turned off the shower on the television set. Now, will you please turn off the shower in the bathroom?" I asked.

Charlie frowned and said, "You should say what you mean."

I sighed and again asked Charlie to turn off the shower in the bathroom. Granted, I could have done that task in a second and saved the frustration. But, Charlie was gradually losing a lot of motor memory and I wanted him to do simple tasks to try to preserve that memory for as long as possible.

Charlie reluctantly went into the bathroom but I could still hear the shower running. I went in to the bathroom and said, "Charlie, please turn off the shower. You left the water running."

"No, I didn't," Charlie responded.

"Charlie please turn off the shower, please," I coaxed.

"Okay." Charlie reached in and turned off the shower.

"Now, you need to change your shirt, Charlie."

"I like this shirt."

"Charlie, your shirt sleeve is all wet from where you turned off the shower."

"Yeah, the TV made it all wet."

You simply cannot reply to that kind of irrational thinking. I thought for a moment and then, I thought of a way I could send Charlie off to group with a smile. Charlie was engaging in magical thinking. He had confused the shower on the TV with the bathroom shower. He'd pulled a sort of switcheroo in his mine.

"Charlie?"

"Yeah?"

"Your mind is becoming quite magical."

"Thank you," my husband said.

"Charlie?'

"Yeah?"

"We need to hurry. Your ride will be here soon."

"Can I tell him about being a magician?"

"Sure," I responded, buttoning up the new, dry shirt I had gotten out of the closet. "You're a regular Houdini," I added as Charlie headed out the door.

"I'm a magician!" Charlie yelled to his driver as he headed toward his ride.

Life is a series of natural and spontaneous changes. Don't resist them – that only creates sorrow. Let reality be reality. Let things flow naturally forward in whatever way they like. Lao Tzu

6.

THE PERSISTENT SHOPPER

Reinforcement in a Troubling Outing

If you cannot leave your loved one at home alone anymore, you will be placed in awkward and frustrating situations in which behaviors need to be overlooked. At the same time, despite the frustration, we caregivers need to look for opportunities for our loved ones to have feelings of success, simply because they attempt to engage in behaviors that most of us take for granted.

Charlie and I went to Target to get a few of the week's supplies. Normally, I go shopping by myself when Charlie is in his day care group. If I take Charlie with me, he strays and gets lost in the store, and my trying to locate him consumes far more time than my day allows. At other times, my shopping cart ends up at the checking line with items I'll eventually sell for a ninety percent reduction at a garage sale.

"Charlie, what is on your shopping list today?"

"I have two things," my husband replied. Charlie took out his list and he headed down an aisle."

"Charlie, that's not the right aisle for lip balm. That's the toy aisle."

"Okay," Charlie replied as he proceeded to check out the toys. I went to him and placed his arm on the shopping cart as I turned it around. "Please hang on to the side of the cart," I requested as I steered him toward the aisle with the lip balm."

I pointed to the rack in which Charlie's usual lip balm was displayed. He checked out each and every package, lifting it from the display and checking it out. There were fourteen different selections we could have made.

After four or five minutes of watching Charlie, I became impatient and said, "Charlie, here's the blue one. You always get the blue one."

Charlie received the package I gave him and studied it as if he were proofreading a book. Then, he said, "It doesn't say SPF 15 on it. This isn't the right one."

"They probably all have an SPF factor, Charlie. They probably just changed the packaging a bit. Let's just get this one."

"No. It has to say SPF 15."

"Do you know what SPF is, Charlie?" Right away, I bit my lip, knowing I should not have placed my husband in that position. I tried to redo what I'd just said.

"Charlie, almost all the lip balms have a good Sun Protection Factor in it now. They don't always say it. This one is the flavor you like."

Charlie again inspected the package and then rejected it. "It doesn't say SPF 15. I don't want it."

"Well, how about one of these other ones then? This one says SPF 20," I suggested.

"No, it has to be blue and it has to say SPF 15."

"They don't have that here, Charlie." We had now been at the lip balm display for about fifteen minutes.

"Okay, we'll go somewhere else then," Charlie said matter-of-factly.

"I don't think so," I replied in an agitated manner.

"You shouldn't have taken me somewhere that they don't have a blue SPF 15, you know."

"Charlie, what else is on your list besides lip balm? I'll pick that up for you somewhere else."

"Mouthwash. I have to have the one in green."

"Yes, I know, Charlie." I led my husband down two aisles as he held onto the cart. I pointed to the bottle of mouthwash he generally used and I picked it up and handed it to him.

Charlie studied the bottle intensely, turning it from the front to the back label. He set it back down on the shelf.

"Charlie, that's your regular mouthwash. Don't you want it?"

"Nope."

"Why don't you want the mouthwash, Charlie?"

"It doesn't say SPF 15 on it."

I had to smile at that one. I looked directly at Charlie and said, "Charlie, that's mouthwash. They don't put an SPF ingredient where the sun don't shine."

"What?" my confused husband asked.

"Charlie, I think I'll get the mouthwash for myself."

Charlie studied me as I put the mouthwash in the cart. Then he shook his head as if chastising me.

"What?" I asked.

"It doesn't have an SPF 15 you know."

"I can live with that, Charlie." I knew that by the time we got home, the SPF 15 factor would be a memory long gone.

As I loaded the trunk with our supplies and then buckled Charlie's seatbelt, I said, "Charlie, you know what?"

"No."

"I think you are one of the most persistent shoppers I've even known."

"Thank you." Charlie had another big smile on his face. "Can we stop for ice cream?"

"That's another trip, Charlie," I commented.

"No, this is this trip."

"Charlie, not only are you a persistent shopper, you're a wonderfully persistent requester as well."

"Thank you."

Sometimes, when you stop for a moment, acknowledge your own negative feelings and then, look for an opportunity to reinforce effort in your loved one, you might end up learning that there's a lot more to your own personality than you previously thought!

7.

THE FAITHFUL FAMILY WATCHDOG

Reinforcing Intention

My son David was at our house attending to some computer repairs for me and Charlie was getting restless. He sat in his recliner chair staring at our son and I could tell it was beginning to unnerve the poor man. Many was the time when I would close the door separating my office from the great room where Charlie watched television. Oftentimes, my husband would turn from the television program and stare into my office for long periods of time and eventually, it would get to me. I'd cease my work and go sit by my silent husband.

On this particular occasion, I had decided it best to simply remove Charlie from the house rather than risking having him stare at my son working on the computer. My son had said the updates and repairs could take an hour or more and Charlie was not going to allow my son to proceed undisturbed.

I asked Charlie if he'd like to go out for an early dinner and then, take a ride. Naturally, he was delighted by the suggestion. Eating was his hobby and he still did it well, with an occasional Heimlich maneuver applied for choking incidents.

After changing my clothes and checking on Charlie, I saw him headed to the office where our son was working. I asked, "Charlie, do you need to go to the bathroom before we leave?"

Charlie answered, "Yes, because I won't be wearing my hat."

Our son gave me the "What!" expression and I simply shrugged. Things like that were routine in our house and lately, I'd thought nothing of illogical and irrational responses.

I locked the front door and asked Charlie to get into the car but he headed instead toward my office. I could hear talking from the area of my office and I didn't want Charlie to keep interrupting our son. Later, the computer expert in the family told me that Charlie had asked him, "Will you be able to find your way out of the house if we leave?" We both thought it was simply precious.

On the way to the restaurant, Charlie seemed concerned.

"Is something on your mind, Charlie?" I asked.

"No."

"Are you thinking about something?" I asked. Sometimes, a probe must be delivered two or three times in different words in order to make sense.

"Why is David using your computer?" Charlie asked.

"He's fixing the computer, sweetheart. He has his own computer."

"I thought so. He should use it then, not yours."

"Charlie, David is fixing the computer, not using it for his personal needs. That's a good thing, Charlie. I don't know how to fix it."

27

"Okay. We'll let him out when we get home."

"Charlie, you're really a wonderful family watchdog, you know."

"Thank you."

"You're welcome."

"You didn't lock the doors."

"Yes, Charlie, I did lock the front door."

"Then David can't get out."

"He can go out the garage door. He knows the code, Charlie."

"I don't."

"That's okay. You have me."

"Okay, I'll watch over you too."

Obviously, Charlie was engaging in irrational thought processing. There is not a lot a caregiver can do as attempts to correct only aggravate the confused mind. So as caregivers, we must look beyond performance and gravitate toward the intention of our loved ones. Charlie's intention was honorable; he wanted to assure the safety of family. In any situation, that intention requires a good word.

I have found that if you love life, life will love you back.
Arthur Rubinstein

8.

THE EXPERT NIGHT FINDER

Responding to Nighttime Confusion

Charlie was now getting up in the night. It was not an every night occasion but it happened frequently enough to disturb my sleep. Thus far, he had not wandered outside the house. But, Charlie would turn on all the lights and I could hear the noise of his wanderings through my bedroom door.

On one particular night, I woke up to noise and saw bright lights all over the house. I went outside and Charlie was looking in the kitchen and the laundry room.

"Charlie, what do you need?" I asked. I had learned some time back not to ask what Charlie was doing. Rather I would ask what he needed, hoping I could somehow pacify him and return him to bed.

"A paper," Charlie answered. He had a look of great concern upon his face and I knew this had to be something triggered during his sleep. It was something profound enough to awaken him and make him wander.

"Okay. Is there something special on the paper?" I asked.

"Yes. It's some writing," Charlie responded.

"Do you know what the writing looked like?"

"Yeah, it looked like writing."

"Did it have numbers, Charlie?"

"Maybe."

"Did you write it recently?' I asked.

"Somebody did." Okay, we were not getting anywhere. So I said, "Charlie, I'll bet it was somebody's phone number."

"Whose?" Charlie asked. I had that one coming.

"Some number you wanted to remember, probably."

"I forgot it."

I was tired and annoyed and trying to think of a way to end the conversation and get Charlie back to bed.

"Oh, Charlie, I think I remember now!" I said with a look of realization. At least, it was as genuine a look as I could produce at three in the morning.

"I don't."

"I know, Charlie. We sometimes misplace things but now I remember. I wrote a note to remind you to bring the cookies for group in the morning. You go back into bed and I'll bring the note to you. You can put it right next to you so you'll see it in the morning."

Charlie looked confused but he headed back to the bedroom. I quickly wrote a reminder note for cookies on a sticky note and took it in to Charlie.

"See, here it is, Charlie. It was hidden under the placemat on the table. It's no wonder you couldn't find it."

"I did find it. Here it is," Charlie said, holding up the paper I had just given to him.

I tucked in my husband and turned out the lights. I kissed him on the top of his head and said, "Charlie, you're an expert night finder."

"I know."

And I returned to bed only to experience a sleepless night. But, Charlie was calm and he slept through the night. My Charlie just loved reassurances of his abilities while the world around him became a maze.

You will never be happy if you continue to search for what happiness consists of. You will never live if you are looking for the meaning of life. Albert Camus

9.

THE GOOD HAND-HOLDER

Two of the older grandchildren had been over most of the day raking for me. I told them we'd all go out to dinner together to celebrate the nineteen bags of leaves they'd managed to secure out on the curb.

I got Charlie ready and the four of us set out for dinner. We decided on the way to go to a favorite pizza restaurant where delicious Italian food was served. Afterwards, we would go to a shop where one of my other granddaughters worked serving ice cream on the weekends.

The two granddaughters and I talked nonstop about school and extracurricular school activities. The oldest was a high school junior and the younger one was a freshman. College applications for the senior had already been put in and accepted and the senior granddaughter was feeling pretty spunky and talkative. Charlie was content to listen. Every once in a while, one of the girls would direct a comment to Charlie and he seemed pleased with the attention. The girls were a natural at accepting Charlie's deteriorating physical and mental condition and their routine acceptance of their grandfather simply warmed my heart.

The two girls had ordered several entrees and could not eat everything so we got a to-go box for them to take home the leftovers. The younger granddaughter said she'd take the box to the car while the rest of us headed to the ice cream shop in the same center. Then, my younger granddaughter indicated she'd forgotten where we parked so I headed out to the street and across to the parking area to show her the way to the car.

Apparently, Charlie had seen me make the turn and he headed into the street, narrowly missing a car that was driving around looking for a parking spot. Without the slightest hesitation, the oldest granddaughter ran to take Charlie's hand saying, "No Poppy, we don't go out into the street without looking for cars." She then steered her Poppy back onto the sidewalk and headed him toward the ice cream parlor. When I looked back, the eighteen year old was holding her grandfather's hand and talking with him like a parent would talk with a younger child. It was such a natural thing and such a beautiful moment for me, just knowing the level of awareness and acceptance of that young adult.

After chatting briefly with the granddaughter serving ice cream and then having our own treats, we dropped the two granddaughters off at their home, I told Charlie I had seen him holding hands with our granddaughter and I'd thought it was such a sweet gesture.

"Yeah," Charlie commented. "You really have to watch them. They could go out right into the street. There could be cars coming."

"Is that what Lindsay told you?" I asked.

"Yeah, I had to pull her out of the street and hold her hand so she wouldn't get hurt."

"Oh, Charlie, you're such a good hand-holder."

"I know."

Charlie walks stooped over, restricting his view. And then, he shuffles his feet, causing him to lose his balance on occasion. I was just grateful we had such an alert and caring hand-holder in the family.

At times, the opportunity for reinforcement comes when the dementia patient transfers the actions of someone else to him/herself. Since your loved one has actually realized that the action was correct, it is not essential that the loved one actually performed the action. The realization of correct behavior is a great opportunity to reinforce.

Life isn't about finding yourself. Life is about creating yourself. George Bernard Shaw

10.

Making Love on Scrabble

Reinforcing Effort

One day in the moderate stages of Charlie's disease, my husband was exhibiting anxious behaviors which suggested he might need mental stimulation. In past years, we had liked to play board games together but I knew that his current abilities would require an adaptation to the Scrabble rules if we were both to play. I elected not to keep score. We simply chose alphabet tiles and tried to make words. We both turned our tiles so the letters showed.

This is the actual board that Charlie and I used the first time we attempted to play. I began by making the word **BOASTED** right down the center of the board. I figured it gave Charlie several opportunities for words using either the vowels or the consonants.

"What should I do?" Charlie asked.

"We're going to make words, Charlie. You have the letters Q, F, H, A, E and S. Can you put them by one of my letters to make a word?"

"Maybe."

I smiled at Charlie and put out the F. Then I said, "We could make DO or we could make…." I ran my finger up the word I had made until my finger was by the O.

Charlie studied the letters diligently and I wondered if he would be able to get the concept he had so skillfully mastered prior to the onset of his disease. He picked up the F and placed it next to the O, just below the B. I smiled and said, "Wow, Charlie, that's a great word! The letter F is sometimes hard to use."

"I know F words," Charlie replied.

"Yes, I remember but it's not your turn now, Charlie; it's my turn." I spelled out the word TESTING, thinking it might give Charlie more letters to work with. I was unsure as to whether I might have confused him by making another lengthy word.

"Mine won't spell anything," Charlie said.

"You can always take more letters, Charlie."

Charlie searched through the letters and took an O and the letters I and a B. He was really concentrating hard on the board. Finally, he asked, "Can you go sideways?"

"You can go any way you want, Charlie. But, it needs to spell a word."

Charlie smiled and put an O underneath the T in TESTING. I was so proud of him! I touched his hand and smiled (positive reinforcement) and then concentrated on my own tiles. I elected to choose some more as I had very few left.

"You have too many letters," Charlie said as he frowned at my tiles. That gave me valuable information. The fewer tiles Charlie had on his side the better.

"Okay, you're right. I'd better get rid of some of them, Charlie." I used the A in BOASTED as an end letter and spelled TRIVIA out to the left side of the board. By making longer words, I was hoping to create the opportunity for Charlie to be successful. I said the word TRIVIA out loud and Charlie said, "We do that in our group. We do that trivia. I can do that. I can do a trivia."

"But, Charlie, can you take that word I made and go up or down and make another word with your letter tiles?" Charlie studied his letters and seemed a bit stumped. He reached over and took three more letters and studied them.

After a moment, I reached out and took the letter I and the letter P and set them away from the other letters. He again studied the word TRIVIA and he smiled. He put his letters below the R and he spelled RIP. Again, I learned something. Charlie had still maintained some spelling ability but we needed to make it manageable by putting out only tiles he could actually use.

At one point, Charlie spelled the word ED. Even though proper names are not really allowed according to the rules of the game, I was pleased that Charlie was now searching out opportunities. When I asked, "Ed?" Charlie explained, "It's someone I know. When he later spelled out BOB, he immediately offered, "It's someone I know." Charlie placed the letter M on the board under the letter I and explained he had intended to spell "I'm. You just have to pretend there's a dash there," he explained. I had no problem with his creativity as his investment in the game was highly rewarding for us both.

We continued that way for over half an hour. The most difficult word Charlie spelled was a three-letter word but he was participating and feeling good about himself. At one point after I had spelled out WOOF, Charlie attempted to put the letters K, C and U immediately after the letter F. I simply removed them from the board (ignored the negative behavior), placed them back in the box (distraction) and told Charlie he should look at his letter H and see if he could make a word (redirect to a positive behavior). He made the word HE and I told him I liked that word because it reminded me of him.

I was almost ready to quit when I had used my letter W as well as two letters O. I yawned and told Charlie I was about out of ideas. He frowned and said, "I want to use my letters and then we can quit."

Charlie had the letters O, L, V and a blank tile. I studied the board and then had an idea. I took away the blank tile and interchanged the letters L and O. Charlie studied the board and asked, "Oh, do they fit somewhere?"

I ran my hand down my original word BOASTED until I got to the letter E. I looked down at Charlie's three tiles and said, "Hmmm, I wonder if they'd fit here, Charlie.'

Charlie looked from the E on the board to the three tiles on the table. He looked up and down again and then grinned from ear to ear! He placed the L and the O and the V in front of the E.

"Charlie, you made a wonderful four letter word!" I said as I patted his hand.

"But I have a tile left," Charlie said.

"That doesn't count," I said. "It's blank."

"Somebody forgot to put the letter on, huh?" Charlie observed.

"What word did you make, Charlie?" I asked.

"You helped me some," Charlie replied.

"Only a little. So read the word, Charlie."

"It's LOVE," he said with a big grin. "It's love! We made love on Scrabble!" he said as he touched my left hand.

And so, we did................................

I told Charlie it was time to pack up the game and he said, "Wait!" He reached over to my remaining tiles and took the letters L and U. He placed them above the letter V in the word TRIVIA.

I was unsure what to say so I sighed and said, "That's really nice, Charlie."

"I know how to make love on Scrabble lots of ways, don't I?" he asked with more eagerness than I'd seen in some time.

"Yes, Charlie, you just might be a Master," I remarked.

Charlie had experienced a very good night and he woke up happy the following morning as well.

When our loved ones are no longer able to play by the rules of the game, there is no reason that the game can no longer be played. Simple consideration of our loved ones' limitations can be opportunities for our own creative minds to get to work. If we can adapt common experiences to the remaining skills of the progressive dementia patient, then we may promote a feeling of efficacy, despite limitations. When you adapt a pleasurable experience to be manageable for the loved one, those rewards carry positive feelings of continued participation in an increasingly elusive environment.

Find a place inside where there's joy, and the joy will burn out the pain. Joseph Campbell.

11.

THE WONDERFUL CONVERSATIONALIST

The mail tuck had just come and Charlie went out to get the mail. I went out to receive the mail from Charlie as he oftentimes throws letters away. Sometimes, he shreds them before I get a chance to open them and that makes bill-paying a real challenge at our house.

About an hour later, Charlie looked out the window and saw the mail truck on the other side of the street. He hurried out the door as quickly as his legs would allow and he crossed the street without looking for traffic. By then, the mail truck was at the next house and Charlie hurried to catch it. I ran out of the house realizing that Charlie had put aside his own safety needs while running after the mail truck. I tailed behind Charlie as it took me a minute to try to ascertain what Charlie was doing. Finally, it dawned on me that he'd forgotten the mail carrier had already delivered the mail and he thought we'd been passed by.

I caught up to Charlie as he was giving the mail carrier a piece of his mind.

"You shouldn't go by people who have lived here so long," Charlie was arguing. The carrier looked confused and asked where Charlie lived. Charlie pointed across the street and gave the mail carrier the family name.

The mail carrier was about to respond when I flashed the card I carried in my pocket on most occasions. "My husband is memory-impaired," it said.

41

Finally, we got a smile out of our mail carrier and she said, "Oh my, I must have forgotten to give you this." She handed Charlie a booklet of advertising and then said, "No bills for you today, thank goodness."

"You should get back to work now," Charlie said as he looked at the flyer.

I nodded and gave our mail carrier a smile of appreciation as I took Charlie's hand and headed home. "Man, Charlie, I haven't seen you move that fast in quite a while."

"I had to. Sometimes the new ones don't know where they're supposed to deliver," Charlie explained. "But I told her what she did wrong and she did the right thing."

I wanted to respond that the woman had been our mail carrier for several years but that would only confuse Charlie. "The right thing?" I asked.

"Yeah, she gave me the mail she forgot to bring me. I told her and she gave it to me."

"Charlie, you always were good at getting things across to people," I replied, not knowing for sure what to say.

But Charlie took it as a reinforcement.

"Thank you," he said. "I was born to be a good talker."

I flashed back to times when Charlie had literally taken my breath away with conversation. He was so knowledgeable and so adept at phrasing his conceptualizations. It made me think that conversation must still be something valuable to him and that he just may have some recollection of early success in linguistics. I made a note to reinforce him whenever he was currently able to get his needs understood verbally. It was such a simple thing and yet it was something that made Charlie feel good.

When our loved ones are stricken with dementia, they continue to hold memories of times in which their brains functioned efficiently and effectively. As caregivers, we need to remember that those skills are treasured memories and we need to look for opportunities to catch our loved ones in the act of engaging in those skills. We're not looking for perfect performance. We only want some semblance of the former skill to manifest.

Positive anything is better than negative nothing.

Elbert Hubbard

12.

The Unknown Bracelet Trick

A Reinforcing Caregiver Moment

I ordered a bracelet from the Alzheimer's Association. It had a stainless steel plate in front, with a stainless steel link bracelet attached to a clasp which was difficult to get on as well as nearly impossible to get off. On the steel plate was an inscription telling anyone who looked at the plate that Charlie had memory problems. There was a number to call so that anyone attempting to help Charlie could get an accurate medical history, allowing him to receive necessary and immediate assistance.

I had attempted on many occasions to get Charlie to wear the bracelet and he had always resisted. One evening, he agreed to have me put it on him after I explained that it was critical that if he or I fell, we both have information on our bodies that would allow others to help us. I showed him a similar bracelet I had ordered for myself, stating that I was an Alzheimer's caregiver. In case I was in need of medical attention and could not give information, Charlie would immediately be identified as someone in need of assistance as well.

The following morning after Charlie had been picked up for his adult day care program, I went into his bedroom. There on the dresser was the bracelet. A link of the chain had been broken, although the clasp remained intact. I could not see how Charlie had the means to get the bracelet off as there were no tools which might have separated the chain anywhere in the vicinity of the bedroom.

I took the bracelet out to my garage workshop, hoping to use the pliers to force the chain link together so that I could convince Charlie to wear it again. Despite my years in the workshop, I could not force the link back together. It continued to puzzle me that my husband had removed such a sturdy chain, seemingly without any tools whatsoever.

My son David came over to visit that afternoon and he also attempted to force the chain link back to its intended position. He was not able to complete the task with my tools, so he took the bracelet home. After a couple of days had passed, David emailed me that he had finally been successful in repairing the chain, using the heavier tools in his own home workshop.

When my son returned the bracelet, intact and with the clasp open, he asked me how Charlie had been able to get the bracelet off. I explained that I was clueless. I had asked Charlie as well and he said he couldn't remember. I understood he had told the truth, the whole truth and nothing but the truth.

I finally convinced my husband that our bracelets needed to remain on at all times. I had difficulty closing the "fool-proof" clasp on

45

Charlie's wrist but once it was on, Charlie seemed to adapt to the wrist decoration. He asked several more times in the next two weeks to have the bracelet removed and I simply said, "No, we're not going to do that, Charlie."

I continued to be frustrated that Charlie might again attempt to remove the bracelet so I periodically attempted to inquire about his hidden skills in bracelet removal.

Charlie seemed to study my question about the bracelet removal and finally he said, "We don't know everything."

At first, I thought he was being a bit mystical so I asked again if he knew how the bracelet got off his wrist.

"It must be a bracelet trick," Charlie said.

"Oh, I see, the unknown bracelet trick. Well, could you maybe show me the trick again, Charlie?"

"I forgot."

I didn't immediately respond, so Charlie added, "I'm good at that. You forgot to tell me I'm good at that. I'm a good forgetter."

By now, Charlie was expecting to be reinforced and when I failed at my job, he did it for me! If a loved one begins to reinforce a behavior without prompting, it is a good sign that your efforts to promote positive feelings have taken effect. The times of self-reinforcement may be few and far between. But any feedback that suggests your caregiving efforts have been effective is reinforcing to you as the caregiver.

If the reinforcement program begins early in the disease, you will undoubtedly have significant results by the time your loved one reaches the moderate stages of the disease. Any sign that the loved one has incorporated the positive reinforcement idea as a good feeling is a measure of the caregiver's persistence, stamina and endurance. And most assuredly, we caregivers have then set the stage as the disease worsens, knowing we have the trust of those for whom we love and protect.

You've done it before and you can do it now. See the positive possibilities. Redirect the substantial energy of your frustration and turn it into positive, effective, unstoppable determination. Ralph Marston.

13.

The Dementia Cream Expert

One evening Charlie and I were watching the Tampa Bay Rays baseball game. They were on the road, playing the Chicago White Socks. Even though Charlie didn't track what was currently going on in the game, he had trace memories of how to play baseball. Thus, watching a baseball game was still a reinforcing and meaningful activity for him.

When one of the commercials appeared, Charlie stared with intensity at the screen. I could see him struggling to make sense of the ad. The advertisement was for a vaginal cream for postmenopausal women. Charlie got a look of concern on his face. He began to tap his hands on his upper legs, a symptom which signals to me a state of anxiety.

"Charlie, can I help you in some way?" I asked.

"Yeah."

"How can I help you, Charlie?"

"I did a bad thing."

"What bad thing did you do, Charlie?"

"They said you get dementia."

I thought about this for a few moments before realizing that the announcer had said that one of the cautions of using the vaginal cream was that of possible dementia. Somehow, Charlie had extrapolated that any use of creams could give a person dementia.

"Charlie, I don't think you've ever used vaginal cream."

"Huh-uh," Charlie responded as he continued to tap his hands.

"Then, you don't have to worry about getting dementia from the cream they just talked about. Okay?" I added hoping to get the anxiety behaviors reduced.

"But, I used it on my hands a couple of times," Charlie said with a look of consternation on his face.

I went to where my husband sat and I took his anxious hands in my own. Then, I said in a very objective way, "Charlie, that's okay. It's really okay to use hand cream if you need it. It won't give you dementia."

"Good," my husband responded, visibly relaxing. He took a deep breath and said, "I would never want to get dementia. Then, I wouldn't understand anything."

"That's right, Charlie, nobody wants to get dementia."

"So, I won't use that cream anymore," Charlie said, leaning back into his lounge chair.

I smiled at my husband and marveled at how emotions can pervade right through the tangled bundles in his brain. I patted his hand and he smiled at me.

"I won't even use it in my coffee," Charlie said. Then he added, "Just in case."

"That's a very good decision about the cream, Charlie," I said. Well, in reality, it was a good decision for my husband as well as for any male.

Charlie had now forgotten about the cream, but he looked pleased with himself. "Oh-oh," he said, "That guy just struck out. "The Yankees aren't too great this year," he summarized.

At times, a simple reinforcement can stop negative feelings and redirect to the task at hand.

Keep your face to the sunshine and you cannot see a shadow.   Helen Keller

14.

The Ten Day Week

Testing the Reinforcement Program

Charlie had fallen in the bathroom shower. Fortunately, he was not injured but about two weeks after the incident, I noticed what appeared to be water damage on a baseboard in the den which was adjacent to the bathroom.

I tried the simplest thing which was ignoring the problem. But then, it became more pronounced and I realized that the stains were approximately the width of the shower behind the den wall. I removed a section of baseboard and sure enough, it was wet. Water appeared to be leaching through the wall at the bottom of the shower. Since the shower was recessed into the foundation floor, the floor itself could not have been leaking.

An inspection by a local contractor revealed that the grouting had apparently cracked about six inches above the floor and the shower water was leaching into the wallboard and then running down the wall. Eventually, the water found the wallboard in the adjacent den room.

The faulty shower was the only one that Charlie could use. I tried showering him in the main bathroom which has a bathtub shower. Charlie fell trying to get into the bathtub and he pulled on the shower curtain for support, bringing down the curtain rod. He was not injured but I asked that he call me when he wanted to get out of the shower. He did that and as I went to help him out of the tub, Charlie again lost his balance and fell forward against the toilet.

"They didn't make this bathroom right, Charlie commented.

"You are totally right about that, Charlie. They made the bathroom for me but they didn't make it for you." Charlie seemed pleased that he had made a correct conclusion and he beamed.

It didn't take a rocket scientist to conclude that Charlie could not use the main bathroom during the renovation. Charlie had figured it out with brain tangles and all. Additionally, the contractor had explained that the house would be a mess during the renovation. I knew Charlie would be disorganized and highly anxious. I began to look for respite care placement for him.

After researching assisted living facilities online, I went to visit several and finally settled on a place that seemed to have many of the same features and activities as the adult day care group that Charlie currently attended. I made arrangements for his stay and then began to prepare Charlie for the transition.

"Charlie, I need for you to do something really special for both of us."

"Maybe I can do it."

"I need for you to stay at a special place so that we can get the shower fixed."

"I want to stay here."

"Charlie, it's not safe for you here. You fell trying to use the other bathroom shower and the shower you generally use has to be torn down and redone. The good thing is that it will be even better."

"How can a shower get better? It's just water coming down."

"Great question, Charlie! They are going to put a bench in the shower so we can sit down and rest and just let the water pour over us and relax us."

"How big a seat?"

"Oh, the bench? Well, it is big enough for two people."

"Okay."

"Okay, what, Charlie?"

"Okay to the seat."

"But, Charlie, the really important part is that you will be staying at a different place while the shower is fixed."

"No, I'll stay here."

"Charlie, you cannot stay here."

"Will you stay here?'

"Yes, Charlie, I have to be here during the renovation."

"Then, I will stay too. I can help."

It took several days of conversation similar to this to finally get Charlie to agree to stay in respite care. I always called it respite care so that he did not feel he was going to a nursing facility.

On the fifth day of conversation, Charlie asked, "Do they have treats?"

"Yes, they do, Charlie. When I visited, they were passing out treats to the group. The group was singing and having fun."

"I can sing."

"Yes, I know, Charlie, you are a very good singer."

"Not as good as Guy. He's better than me."

"It's not a contest, Charlie. You might even be the best singer in the new group."

"Okay."

"Okay, to what, Charlie."

"I will go sing."

And we had our first breakthrough.

Yesterday is not ours to recover, but tomorrow is ours to win or lose. Lyndon B. Johnson

15.

The Experiment

Generalization of Reinforcement

The day came for Charlie to go to respite care. All arrangements had been made with the contractor to attempt to finish the bathroom in record time. Charlie would be in respite care for eight days while the contractor and his crew worked extra weekday hours and on the weekend as well. I felt myself blessed to have found a crew that would agree to do the work, realizing that it was going to cost a lot extra to have my husband in respite care.

For me, the cost of placing Charlie in the assisted care memory unit was a prudent one. The unit was "secured," meaning once Charlie was in the facility, he could not get out the front door unless escorted by someone authorized to take him out of the facility. Once in the residential portion of the building, Charlie would be free to come and go as he wished. There were several activity areas as well as courtyards where residents could go to socialize or have alone time outside. In addition, Charlie would have his own room, complete with a bathroom.

Even through Charlie had agreed to "go sing," I remained skeptical about his willingness to stay away from home. The respite experiment took a turn for the worse the evening before the bathroom renovation was to occur.

"Charlie, do you need a reminder about what is happening tomorrow? It is something special and it affects both of us."

"What?"

"You won't be going to the Friendship Center tomorrow. Instead, you'll be going to respite care while the bathroom renovation takes place."

"No."

"No, what, Charlie?"

"No, I'm not going there. I will go to my group."

"Charlie, they will have a group at the respite center. They will have activities and they will sing. It's a lot like the Friendship Center."

"Then, I'll just go to the group I always go to if they're the same."

"Charlie, it's just not safe for you to be home while the bathroom is being renovated."

"Why is it being fixed? What is wrong with it?"

Charlie and I had been over this so many time the past two weeks. But, Charlie was very nervous about change and this wasn't the time to argue. Trying to be rational with someone with Alzheimer's disease is next to impossible.

"Charlie, the bathroom is old and it needs to be updated so it will be safe to use. When it's fixed, we can both use the shower, even if we need to use a walker or a wheelchair."

"I won't use a walker."

Okay, I had that one coming. It was just too much information.

"I know, Charlie. But, I need you to do something really special for me. It's really important to me, Charlie." I looked at Charlie, touched him arm and smiled. I was now counting on his motivation to want to please me as best he could.

"What do I have to do?"

"Charlie, it might be one of the most important things you've ever had to do. And I have to do the very same thing."

"What is it?"

"We have to stay the course, Charlie. You have to stay the course at respite care where you can safely use the shower and I have to stay the course at home where there will be fumes and noise and a lot of inconvenience."

"Your course might be harder."

Oh, how I loved that man at that moment! Despite the progression of the disease, he had been able to consider his scenario as well as mine.

"Oh, Charlie, how sweet you are! My course may be difficult but yours is just as important – maybe, even more so."

"I will just eat and sing."

Noticing that eating was again first on Charlie's list of activities, I replied, "Yes, you will do that, Charlie. But, you will also stay the course and that's important."

"Like in the Navy when I didn't want to do something, I had to do it anyway."

"Exactly!" I said, encouraged that Charlie was using the only reference he could come up with at the time. "It's exactly like that, Charlie. We each have to do our own duties, even if we don't want to."

"If we stay the course, what happens then?"

"Good question, Charlie. If we stay the course, we have each done something honorable. We have each done the right thing."

"So, Charlie said with a very serious look on his face, "if I stay the course, the war will probably end?"

"You might say that," I remarked.

"I just did."

The doorbell rang and I knew the contractor and his crew had arrived to begin the demolition. I asked Charlie to check his bag one last time as I escorted the contractor in and talked for about five minutes. I then excused myself and told Charlie we were leaving now.

"Okay," Charlie said. He looked very confused and a bit frightened as well.

I took Charlie's bag and we went outside to get into the car. As usual, after Charlie was seated, I reached over and buckled his seatbelt.

"I'm so proud of you, Charlie," I said

"Okay," he replied.

I took a scenic route to the respite facility, explaining how Charlie's stay would somewhat similar to going to the Friendship Center. The major difference would be that he would have overnights at the respite facility.

"Do I know anybody there?" Charlie asked.

"You will soon, Charlie. You make friends much more easily than I do."

So, that's why I have to go there instead of you, right?"

"Pretty much, Charlie, pretty much."

It is often prudent not to argue with the logic of Alzheimer's patients. If they are willing to attempt a rationalization of an event, then it is generally best to go along with it unless the rationalization is dangerous.

As we drove, I concentrated on opportunities to reinforce Charlie's thinking so that he would maintain a positive attitude. As we got close to the facility, I slowed the car. Charlie looked to the right and saw a large, three story building and said, "Oh no, I'm not going there!"

Immediately, I reached my hand over to his and said, "You are so right, Charlie, you are not going there." I turned into the adjacent building, a one story, pleasant looking building which was landscaped and looked somewhat like a large ranch house.

"This is kinda pretty," Charlie remarked.

"I thought so too, Charlie. And, this pretty place is where you will stay the course while our bathroom is fixed."

"That doesn't look too hard. Are you going to stay the course here too?"

"I wish I could, Charlie. I wish I could stay the course where they feed me and let me doing activities and let me make new friends."

"I can sing there," Charlie said in a matter-of-fact tone of voice.

"Absolutely, you can sing here, Charlie. Now, we need to get out of the car and go in so you can get to meet people."

Much to my amazement and delight, Charlie said, "Okay."

I had done most of the paperwork for the facility the previous week but I would have to sign a few papers before I left to go back home. I pressed the buzzer and was buzzed into the reception area.

Immediately, a woman came to stand in front of us, saying, "Oh, you must be Charlie! We've been waiting for you, Charlie!"

I requested that we see Charlie's room and then said, "Then I have to do some paperwork while you show Charlie around."

Charlie look a bit confused but he followed the attendant. I heard him say, "I am going to stay the course." I followed behind.

The attendant replied, "Oh, I'm so glad to hear that, Charlie. I hear you have a wonderful voice."

"Yeah, I do," Charlie responded.

We were escorted down a corridor and into a small, private room. Charlie was shown the attached bathroom and then, the attendant motioned out the window and commented on the courtyard.

"Can I go out?" Charlie asked.

"Of course you can, Charlie. We want you to explore the place after you've settled in.'

The attendant left and Charlie looked around the room. "No TV," he commented.

"Oh, sure they have televisions, Charlie. They are in the living room. Here, let's get out your clothes and put them in the dresser drawers. Oh, Charlie, look!"

I pointed to the dresser where a balloon floated above a small bag of treats. Charlie headed right for the treats.

"It says, 'Welcome, Charlie!'"

Charlie grabbed the bag of treats and sat in a chair adjacent to the dresser. I snapped a picture of him with a big grin on his face. So far, so good.

We finished unpacking and I then showed Charlie the kitchen, dining room and living room where a large, flat-screened television set adorned the wall. Charlie liked the way the facility was decorated. His corridor had a beach theme and was brightly colored. The decorations were warm and welcoming.

"It's kinda like a house," Charlie commented.

"I thought so too, Charlie."

We then went out to a common area where other residents were milling around talking or engaged in activities. Immediately, an attendant came to us. A resident also came over and asked Charlie, "Were you in the Navy too?"

Charlie was wearing his Navy hat which is oftentimes a social icebreaker. "Yeah," Charlie answered. "Were you too?"

The Navy resident immediately escorted Charlie into another room and they chatted like old friends. It was agreed that this was a good time for me to exit. I leaned in the door where Charlie and his new friend were chatting and blew him a kiss. He blew one back to me and continued to talk. I had never in my wildest dreams imagined anything going more smoothly!

I returned to the reception area, signed a few more papers and then headed home to stay the course.

Charlie's lengthy day care experience had been a relatively smooth and positive experience. Even though he was in the early moderate stages of Alzheimer's disease at the time, I was pleased to learn that the trust in new caregivers had gone relatively smoothly. Charlie's current stay in respite care would now be the ultimate test of whether those feelings of safety and trust would transfer to other caregivers and another environment. Charlie was now decidedly more confused and disoriented than when he had entered the day care program two years previous to respite care. Ideally, generalization to a totally different environment would demonstrate that the reinforcement program was not simply situation-specific.

16.

Long-Distance Reinforcement

Instilling a Sense of Continuity

It is apparent by now that reinforcement can take place simply by agreeing with an Alzheimer's patient. Because their cognitive functioning is confusing and frightening at times, the simple act of having a loved one say, "You're right!" or "I agree with you" can be an act of kindness and solace, resulting in positive feelings.

Charlie's placement in respite care would prove to be a severe challenge to the model of caregiver trust and positive moods I had attempted to instill in him for the past eight years. If staff continued to reinforce Charlie in person while I attempted to continue my own reinforcement plan by phone, Charlie had a much better chance of getting through the current disruption to his life.

The first evening, Charlie and I talked on the phone. Workmen were still at our home and I could not leave. I immediately assessed that Charlie was disoriented.

When I answered the phone, Charlie simply said, "Hi."

"Hi, Sweetheart," I replied. I was tired from all the noise of the day. Workmen had jackhammered through the concrete shower floor and my head was still ringing from the noise.

"Are you coming to get me?" Charlie asked. Okay, this was what I dreaded and it was here already.

"Charlie, you are spending the night there," I replied as simply as I could.

"They didn't pick me up."

That took me aback, but only for a moment as I reoriented to Charlie's brain. "Oh, Charlie, remember, you are attending a different group while the bathroom is fixed. They won't pick you up for a while now. You will sleep there in the room. Have you had any of the treats they gave you?" I asked, hoping to redirect my husband and assuage his disorientation and fear.

"It was good," Charlie replied.

"It *was* good?" I asked in amazement. "You mean, you already ate all the treats they gave you?"

"Maybe. So will you be here soon?"

"Oh, honey, I am so very tired tonight. The workmen have been jackhammering all day and my head really hurts. Could you just stay in your room there tonight?" I asked.

"Why does your head hurt?"

"I think it's from all the jackhammering. And, probably the construction dust too, Charlie. Did you and your new friend Sawyer have a good visit?"

"Who's Sawyer?"

"You met him this morning when you went to the group. He said he was a Navy man too."

"Maybe."

"Okay. I hope you had a good dinner?"

"Did I eat?"

"I think you did, Charlie. I think you went to the dining room and you had your dinner there. Maybe, you can go sing after dinner.'

"Is that when you'll come to get me. If I sing, will you come then?"

"Oh, sweetheart, I am too tired to come tonight. I have to stay the course here." I was hoping the phrase might strike a chord with Charlie.

"Oh. I have to stay the course here."

"Charlie, you are so good to do that for us. You are so good to stay the course there while I stay the course here."

"Yeah, I've been here two weeks now. So I'm really good at staying the course. Oh-oh."

"What's the oh-oh, Charlie?"

"They just told me it's time to go in the room and sing."

"Then you'd better get going, sweetheart. They are depending on you."

"Bye."

"Bye, Charlie. I love y...." But Charlie had already hung up to go sing.

I emailed the staff at the respite care center that night and asked that Charlie and Sawyer be re-introduced in the morning. I got an email back immediately telling me that the men would meet again. The director explained that Sawyer also had severe memory "issues" and that apparently, even though they'd had a great time together that first day, neither had remembered one another once they had parted.

If we caregivers are allowed to hate anything, surely we can hate the disease that deprives our loved ones of basic happiness.

Work hard for what you want because it won't come to you without a fight. You have to be strong and courageous and know that you can do anything you put your mind to. If somebody puts you down or criticizes you, just keep on believing in yourself and turn it into something positive. Leah LaBelle

17.

Renovations of Various Natures

Generalization

It was now the weekend and the tile layer was at our home. I knew him well and trusted him to finish his work while I took a break and got Charlie out of respite care for several hours. I did have some reservations about the outing as our phone conversation the previous evening verified that Charlie remained somewhat disoriented to his immediate environment. But, the staff said he was actually adjusting very well, given his situation, that being a non-permanent resident.

I entered the facility and immediately went back to Charlie's room. He was not there, so I looked around the complex and soon spotted my man, walking the halls, just looking around. He had on his jacket and his Navy hat and had obviously remembered that I was coming to take him out for the day.

After a big hug, I let staff know we were leaving for a few hours and we headed out the door. Charlie was quiet as we approached our car. "Are we going home?" he asked.

"We are going to lunch, Charlie. And maybe afterwards, if we're not too tired, we'll take a ride."

We got into the car and I buckled up Charlie and then, myself. I asked Charlie where we should go for brunch.

"We should go to the place that has sweet potato fries," he responded. He raised his eyebrows in a gesture that was precious. He seemed more relaxed in the car and, almost a bit playful!

I knew exactly where to go so I headed toward the restaurant. I had picked up Charlie at 11 AM so that we could get to a restaurant before the Saturday brunch crowd made things more difficult for us.

After exiting the car, I had to wait for Charlie who was straining to get up. He was already out of practice, so I went to help him rise from his car seat. Then, we walked ever-so-slowly to the door of the restaurant. I asked for a booth near the back so that we would have more privacy and Charlie would be closer to the restroom. As soon as we were seated, he got up to use the restroom. I ordered coffee for Charlie and an iced tea for myself.

When Charlie arrived back from the restroom, I suggested his usual menu items and he quickly agreed that I should order for both of us. After ordering, I asked Charlie about the group singing experience.

"I'm the best singer," he eagerly offered

"That's what I heard, Charlie! Congratulations!"

"Who told you?" There was that paranoia again. I hadn't experienced it for a while but now that the environment had changed, Charlie's suspiciousness returned. I wondered if I would have emotional renovations with Charlie when he returned home.

"Everyone thinks so, Charlie. They say you're the best singer they've had there for quite some time."

"Yeah, that's right."

"So, what kinds of songs do you sing?'

"I don't know. But, they give us a paper with the words on it. All you have to do is sing the words."

I told Charlie about what I did in the house while all the workers were present. Then, I showed him some pictures of the renovation on my cell phone.

"That's a mess."

"It is, Charlie. You are so right. It's the biggest mess we've had at our house since last Christmas!"

"Is it Christmas?"

"Oh, no, Charlie. I'm sorry. I think I confused you. We are having the bathroom fixed and they are tearing up the floor and the walls."

"I could help."

"Charlie, I used to be able to help too. But, I think we've both earned the right to hire strong young men who can do the heavy work."

"Okay. I'm hungry."

"Here they come with our food now."

I tried to initiate conversation but as usual, Charlie only responded with one word or two. I was now used to carrying the conversation for us both. We lingered at the restaurant until I saw a line standing by the door. Charlie had already used the restroom three times and when I suggested we leave, he headed for the bathroom again while I took care of the check.

We struggled back to our car and got Charlie and myself strapped in and then asked Charlie if he'd like to go for a ride.

"Okay," He replied.

By then, I was all talked out so we rode while listening to the radio. I drove toward one of the Keys south of Sarasota. It was a long drive but it was a scenic view which paralleled the Gulf of Mexico. Charlie strained to look at the various sites. He appeared calm and relaxed. We stopped twice to use restrooms.

I stopped at the South Venice Jetty. In past years, Charlie and I had frequently gone to the jetty after dinner. We would stand and watch the dolphin play and occasionally, we would be treated to a mother with a new baby prancing in the Gulf waters. I asked Charlie if we could get out and walk the jetty.

"No, I'm too tired," he replied. For the past year or so, it had been very difficult to get Charlie to walk with me, so I simply let it go.

I drove into the village of Venice and stopped a few feet short of the gelato shop. This time, when I asked Charlie if he wanted to get out and get a gelato, he was eager and he extricated himself from the seat, with some assistance from my right hand. Charlie was requiring more and more physical assistance these days and I vowed to continue my three-times–a-week gym routine.

We both opted for a decadent double chocolate gelato and we savored the taste long after the last bite was taken. I was dead-tired but when I took a prolonged look at my husband, he looked aged and worn. His illness was taking a terrible toll on him and I grieved for what he was missing in our geriatric years. But, I also knew that one of the "blessings" of Alzheimer's disease is that the patient has little to no knowledge of what has been lost.

On the ride back to Sarasota, I talked about the programs Charlie was in at the respite facility but he had no memory of anything but the singing sessions. I asked about Sawyer and Charlie asked "Who is that?" When I arrived home I would again email staff to re-introduce the men.

I was shocked when I drove up to the respite facility and Charlie got out of the car without an argument. He was truly exhausted and he simply wanted to rest. I took him inside and we went to his room. He lay down on the bed and I took off his shoes and tucked him in. It was late afternoon and he would soon be called for dinner. I kissed my man on the cheek and silently left the room and went to the car.

On the way back to the home renovation, I fought tears and at one point in time, I had to pull off the road. *How had it come to this?* I silently asked myself. During the few days that Charlie had been in respite care, I had almost relaxed to the point that I had nearly forgotten the disease of human devastation called Alzheimer's disease. Spending those few hours with Charlie had again triggered emotions that I'd experienced daily when Charlie was at home with me.

Almost as a luxury, I sat in the car in misery for a moment or two and then chastised myself and, instead, engaged in positive self-reinforcement. I had slept through the night for the first time in several years while at home. I would soon have a new bathroom. My husband had willingly gone back to a facility where he was known as the best singer. It would be enough for today. Charlie felt safe and secure in a totally different environment.

I turned my tears to feeling of personal efficacy that the years of reinforcement had resulted in generalization. My husband now trusted others to do what I could not always do for him. Should the time come that I had to relinquish my role of caregiver to that of advocacy, I felt my own feelings just might generalize to the new role as well.

Believe in yourself. Have faith in your abilities. Without a humble but reasonable confidence in your own powers, you cannot be successful or happy.

Norman Vincent Peale

18.

Back Home

Practicing the Program

By this time in the respite care experiment, I was pleased that the positive reinforcement of the past eight years had apparently transferred to another environment. And now, it was time to bring Charlie home. Strangely, this is where the major problems commenced.

For several days following Charlie's return home, whenever I asked him to help with a chore (or to do something fundamental to his own wellbeing), he would respond, "I don't want to,"

I knew Charlie had been pampered in the assisted living facility and that was fine. He deserved the attention for simply staying the course. But, by Charlie's second day at home, his refusal to do basic things such as showering became a source of irritation.

It took a while but finally, I thought I had gotten to the root of Charlie's apparent stubbornness. At most assisted living facilities, residents are told that they have the right to refuse to participate in any activity available at the facility. This includes showering. Charlie had not made the transition back to the living-at-home expectations. This should not have surprised me. What did give me pause to smile was the fact that my husband had no memory of the staff, of the activities of the facility nor of the new friends he had made. But, he had remembered the rights given to him when he first entered the facility.

Charlie and I sat down that night and I told him I was so proud of him staying the course at respite care. He smiled and he said that, yes, he had been very good.

"But, Charlie, you are at home now and things might be a little different."

"Yeah, the cooking here is better," Charlie commented

"But, Charlie, you and I take showers every day when we're at this house.'

"I don't want to."

"I'm sure that's true, Charlie. You are good at telling me what you don't like. But, here's the thing. We always take showers in this house.'

"Is it the law?"

"Well, let's say it's the rule. It's the rule."

"Why? I don't want to."

"It's one of the ways we are kind to one another, Charlie. We keep our bodies clean."

"Okay."

"Okay, what, Charlie?"

"I will shower if it is a rule.'

"Thank you."

And that it was all it took to reorient Charlie. His was a highly concrete world and I had neglected to tell him to change the rules.

For some time, I had to again practice my own program of reinforcement. A simple change in the routine of a loved one can unsettle and disorient them. Both the caregiver and the loved one need to be reminded of the rules of the house.

Our greatest weakness lies in giving up. The most certain way to succeed is always to try just one more time.
Thomas A. Edison

19.

The Amazing Amygdala

When Feelings are Disconnected

Although all of the parts of the brain are essential to normal processing of the environment, none is more important emotionally than the amygdala. This pair of small, almond-shaped tissues lies deep in the brain, close to another organ named the hippocampus. While the hippocampus monitors immediate memory messages, the amygdala is critical to emotional processing. In Alzheimer's disease, both of these brain organs suffer damage fairly early in the neurodegenerative process of Alzheimer's disease.

Fear is one of the prominent feelings that helps guard individuals from potential harm. And of course, positive emotions are also processed in the organ essential to emotional awareness. As Alzheimer's disease progresses, more and more connections are lost between the amygdala and the cortex. Thus, emotions may become either very bland or very intense from the lack of a working relationship with the rest of the brain.

There are those who contend that if a dementia patient was more emotionally expressive or even volatile prior to the onset of the disease, the affective symptoms would only get more intense. Conversely, if the patient was more emotionally contained, s/he may be more emotionally bland after onset of symptoms of dementia. If I were to have used this commonly-held criteria to predict

Charlie's progression of emotions, he would have been expected to become an emotionally-challenging patient.

When working in skilled nursing facilities during the latter years of my clinical practice, I continually noted that many dementia patients appeared relatively calm and cooperative, even though they were no more highly skilled in processing events than those who appeared to be more emotionally volatile. I also noted that the calmer patients appeared to respond well to positive reinforcement from staff.

When my Charlie became mentally compromised, I vowed to attempt a program of positive reinforcement with the hope that, if I started early on in the process when the disease had not overtaken critical parts of his brain, the feelings of pleasure or personal efficacy just might carry over to the latter stages of the disease. Granted, Charlie would fail to remember events, but emotionally, he just might have feelings of safety and trust based on the reinforcement of the primary caregiver.

In the moderate stages of Charlie's disease process, I could see that he continued to respond positively to my reinforcement attempts. Even into the more severe stages, my husband carried a positive attitude in most all social situations, including his day care group. Furthermore, Charlie maintained a positive and grounded feeling of trust in me, his primary caregiver.

Research is now beginning to emerge which tends to support the idea of positive reinforcement early in the dementia process. (Buchanan & Fisher, 2002; Beville, 2010). Additional research further suggests that reinforcement programs may also result in reducing wandering behaviors in dementia patients (Heard & Watson, 1999).

Although the early research is promising, we need extensive studies into all means of helping both Alzheimer's patients and their caregivers through the lengthy and demanding process of the disease.

Start where you are. Use what you have. Do what you can. Arthur Ashe

20.

Learning the A B C's

Of Dementia Reinforcement

In our search for reinforcement clues for dementia patients, we use the following formula:

A = Affect/Emotions

B = Behaviors

C = Cognitions

All of the areas of functioning are critical to reinforcement as, at any given time, an Alzheimer's patient may be stuck in any of the modes of experiencing the environment. If we begin to think in terms of opportunities based upon the A B C's, we will have a much higher probability of being able to find some effective means of reinforcement, even in the most frustrating of situation.

In order to begin to spot such opportunities, let's take a look at the previous stories and divide them by affective, behavioral or cognitive opportunities:

Affective/Emotional: In the story of the Family Watchdog, Charlie actually expressed emotional concern for the wellbeing of a family member. We have to look past the annoying conclusion that he was disregarding the intelligence of the person involved. Instead, we concentrate on the fact that an inappropriate behavioral response had its origin in an emotional concern that was appropriate. Charlie was concerned because if he had been in a foreign environment, he might have been afraid to have been left alone, with no way out. He transferred those feelings of concern to our son and we need to concentrate on the underlying emotion and not on the manner in which that concern was expressed.

In the story of the Hand holder, Charlie was actually rescued by a grandchild when he inappropriately began to walk out into the street. But, he did comply with the grandchild's request to hold her hand and then, he expressed concern for the child's wellbeing. The compliance behavior was secondary in that story, for Charlie's interpretation was that he was concerned for the grandchild. Charlie's interpretation was one of face-saving and that also is an emotional component to the story.

Making Love on Scrabble was a prime example of how behavioral, cognitive and emotional experiences can merge in multiple potential to reinforce. The end result was that Charlie stuck with the game despite his cognitive deficits. One could choose to reinforce that behavioral aspect. Charlie also tried his best to use limited cognitive skills to engage in the task so we could also reinforce his ability to spell the simple words. But for me, the overriding component was that Charlie recognized a word that epitomized our relationship and he was exuberant in expressing his own delight. Thus, it was easy to give a reinforcement for the affective component, with implied reinforcement for the cognitive and behavioral elements as well.

Behaviors: The Very Best Frog Catcher in the World is a prime example of pure behavioral success. After having difficulty understanding my needs about the frog removal, Charlie was able to coordinate his physical movements and remove the frog in order to take it to a less annoying environment, the nearby preserve. My reinforcement of his behavior resulted in obvious feelings of efficacy for Charlie.

In the Persistent Shopper, Charlie's behaviors were aggravating my needs to get chores completed. But, by not allowing his behaviors to become the focus of my attention, he was eventually able to help with the task. In fact, he briefly appeared to have taken in (cognitively) some of my feedback about name brands. And, eventually, his feelings about the experience were positive because of this cognitive connection to the experience.

While Charlie was in respite care, his pleasant behaviors continued and staff gave ample positive reinforcement. Charlie had no breakdowns in behavioral functioning which might be expected with a dementia patient who experiences a new environment. Charlie did experience cognitive disorientation but that would happen in any new environment. The fact that Charlie was able to "stay the course" without significant incidents was a validation of the years of trust-building.

When Charlie returned to our home following respite care, his behaviors temporarily deteriorated as a result of his recent privileges of being able to refuse participation in activities (including bathing). However, the trust between us was sufficient that when Charlie understood that different rules apply in different places, his behavior was then reinforced.

Cognitive: When loved ones exhibit cognitive confusion, there is sometimes an opportunity to reinforce the cognitive abilities or ideas which eventually emerge. In the story of The Creative Interpreter, when Charlie commented that what I had said was news to him, his response was delivered in such a pleasant manner that I commented on his creativity. Even though Charlie probably had an idea of just how his creativity oftentimes frustrated me, he took the comment as a compliment and carried it with him.

In The Mental Magician chapter we turned his confusion and his strange interpretations of a shower image into a positive cognitive image ignoring the negative behavior and instead, concentrating on how he had apparently performed a magical act. Charlie did attempt to explain (problem-solve) something that was a puzzle to me, so a cognitive reinforcer was in order.

The Night Finder is much easier interpretation which then allowed for reinforcement. Charlie told me what he wanted and I simply reinforced his ability to do that. And, of course, when Charlie defined himself as "a good forgetter," his mental creativity was reinforced.

Knowing is not enough; we must apply. Willing is not enough; we must do. Johann Wolfgang von Goethe

21.

Practice Makes Patience

There is an old saying that "Practice Makes Perfect." We've probably all heard the phrase in elementary school. But as caregivers of dementia patients, we all understand that no matter how hard our loved ones try, they simply cannot reach a state of perfection in affective, behavioral or cognitive functioning. However, we caregivers **can** practice our responses. If we practice a routine of delayed responses while looking for opportunities for reinforcement, we will gradually produce a level of patience that surprises us.

We caregivers are entitled to our intense feelings of anger, frustration, anxiety and helplessness. Non-caregivers simply cannot imagine the warped world in which we live our daily lives. But, as the saying goes, "The definition of insanity is doing the same thing again and again and expecting different results." Our loved ones will **not** get better. But, **we** can get better at managing our reactions to situations which are simply not within our control.

In order to begin the practice routine, we must first believe change can be accomplished. We must also believe that we are capable of changing our own reactions to the frustrating feelings, actions and thoughts of our loved ones. We must challenge ourselves to stop, look and listen. We must stop our own reactions, look at the faces of our loved ones for clues and then, listen to the messages actually being conveyed to us.

In order to stop our own negative reactions, we must actively stop ourselves in the process. The first few times, our success rates may not be very high as we have already patterned our own reactions to the negative situations which result from the decline of our loved ones.

When I say stop, I literally mean STOP! You can tell when your heart pounds and your blood pressure races and you want to get away to save yourself. You know that feeling. So, when it occurs, stop in midsentence, take deep breaths and even walk away if you must.

Give yourself enough time to say (and to believe) that you will now look for goodness in your loved one. Acknowledge your own feelings and then, go back to the issue. This time, listen to the loved one. S/he may be flailing verbally but listen, without responding. An argument simply cannot occur if two people are not participating.

Listen for fear in your loved one. Listen for confusion. Confusion and fear may be camouflaged in accusations and put-downs. But they arise from fear and confusion and not from hatred of or disappointment in you. If a loved one is out of control, s/he is almost always giving the receiver vital information about him/herself. **When you allow your own emotions to become the focus of the exchange, you have lost a valuable opportunity to learn more about your loved one.**

If a loved one accuses you of treating him/her like a child, there is fear there, fear of becoming childlike, fear of becoming dependent. If a loved one accuses you of stealing or hiding things, that is vital information about the true disorganization of the mind. If a loved one suddenly gets out of control and accuses you (or others) of inappropriate deeds, it is a window into the soul of the quagmire of Alzheimer's, or Lewy Body, or frontal lobe dementia, or vascular dementia or of any other type of progressive dementia.

So, if our loved ones are actually offering glimpses into the personal feelings of the degradation and humiliation of their own disease, why would we even want to retaliate? Because accusations are hurtful, that's why. And we aren't used to being hurt in that way from someone with whom we have had a loving relationship with for years.

My contention is that, as strong as the urge is to "make things right," you simply cannot go into battle with an unarmed bystander. And if we caregivers know anything, it is that our loved ones have lost their armor, their weapons and their ammunition as well as their ability to engage in the battles this world has thrust before them.

Of course, that is a disappointing realization. It is not what we planned together. But it is reality. And reality contains one of the best opportunities we have to engage in personal growth. So: STOP your own negative reactions, LOOK at the fear and confusion in your loved one and LISTEN to an opportunity to offer solace to one who is hurting.

Problems are not stop signs; they are guidelines.
Robert H. Schuller

22.

Lions and Tigers and Bears
Preparing for Mind-Set Change

There is probably not one of us that would not want to be armed if we were walking the woods and a lion or tiger or bear appeared in front of us. But, if we fail to prepare for the changes in our loved ones, we caregivers are walking into danger, unarmed. And if we fail to realize that sixty percent of caregivers are victims to death prior to the deaths of the loved one for whom we are caring, we have little idea of even having entered the battle. It is not a battle against our loved ones. Rather, it is a battle to preserve ourselves while still offering respect and kindness to those walking toward an uncertain death.

I will continue to use Charlie as an example as Charlie's thoughts, feelings and actions are a composite of what is experienced by the majority of those who attempt to cope with a neurodegenerative condition such as Alzheimer's disease.

Put yourself right into this discussion, imagine how you might feel and then, back away and listen:

"You took my best shirt and now, I have to wear something I hate!"

"Charlie, what do you need?"

I offer no response to the accusation but I am already in a problem-solving mode.

"I need my shirt and you took it! You probably threw it away. You always hated that shirt.....just like you hate me!"

I take a couple of deep breaths as Charlie's unfounded statements initially angers me. I begin to look Charlie in the face and I see fear because he cannot find his favorite shirt.

"Charlie, I think you really like that shirt. Shall we look together or maybe you'd like an iced tea while I look for the shirt?"

Charlie is frustrated and getting out of control. Loss of emotional control signals that cognitive disorganization will get even more intense so I want to remove the emotional component as quickly as possible. Charlie is telling me that his mind is disordered and that he fears I will no longer love him because of his deficits. I do not respond to the inappropriate cognitive and affective components. I have to change a mind-set that is accustomed to dealing with rational conversation. So, instead of reacting, I have Charlie define the problem and then, I offer to help. I also offer to have Charlie cool down and separate himself from his own confusion and frustration.

"Can I watch tv?"

"Sure, I'll turn it on for you, Charlie."

"Okay."

I go back into the kitchen and get a glass of iced tea for Charlie. I bring it to him and then say, *"Charlie, I like the way you told me exactly what you need. I'll go look now."*

This was a brief conversation for purposes of example, but let's now extend the discussion as it could have gone.

"You took my best shirt and now, I have to wear something I hate."

"I did not! Charlie, I don't much appreciate you accusing me of things I didn't do!"

"Yes, you did! You keep putting things where I can't find them."

"I put your shirt in your drawer, Charlie. That's where it always is. Now, go find it. I'm busy making dinner."

"See, you never own up to your own problems! You take things and you never put them back. You're the one with the problem! You're the one who always tries to confuse me."

"That's just plain rude, Charlie. And it's not true either. Just look at all the things I do for you. And, I never get any thanks for any of it! You don't appreciate anything I do for you and I'm sick of it!"

Now, this is an argument that could easily escalate and go on for hours. As a caregiver, I am trying to defend my own helping traits while I accuse Charlie of being ungrateful for my attempts to help him with things he can no longer do for himself. **You simply cannot engage in a rational argument with someone with a compromised brain**. But, that's what most of us do until we stop, look and listen. We begin to look for things that are unfair and we feel the need to defend ourselves from false accusations. It is an effort in futility.

Talking with those with uncompromised cognitive functioning has become so commonplace in our own minds that we have developed mind-sets that are actually nonfunctional with the compromised brain of our loved one. Our loved ones will not change; they will get worse. It is we who must change the way we think about interactions and what we want to accomplish from those interactions. And, if we cannot do that, we need to think about relinquishing that responsibility to others. There is no shame in acknowledging that you do not believe you have it in you to develop new mental skill sets. There is sadness in affirming that you cannot be everything you wanted to be for your loved one.

The joy of life comes from our encounters with new experiences and hence, there is no greater joy than to have an endlessly changing horizon, for each day to have a new and different sun. Christopher McCandless

23.

The Peculiar Clock

Choosing a Fork in the Road

It was just after noon. To be exact, it was 12:25 PM on a Sunday in mid-October. I had just finished putting the last of the luncheon plates in the dishwasher. I then went into the family room to check on Charlie who was watching a football game. As soon as I entered the room, he said:

"When are you going to fix our dinner?"

I was taken aback but I answered, "Charlie, we just had lunch. It's not time for dinner yet."

I had stated a fact but Charlie was not pacified with the answer.

"You're crazy! Look, my watch says its five o'clock. I'm hungry and its dinnertime."

I went to Charlie, looked at his face and then, noted that he appeared confused. I picked up his wrist. Looking at the position of the watch on his hand, I was able to ascertain that the watch was not upside down. I pondered the source of his confusion before answering.

"Charlie that must be a strange watch you have on today."

"It's not strange. You're the one that's strange. You should be getting our dinner ready."

I went to the laundry room and took off the large clock on the wall. I took the clock to Charlie and then said, "Charlie, let's use this clock. It always tells the correct time."

Charlie looked at the clock and said, "It looks like five o'clock on that one too. You better get going. You're running late."

Now, I knew for sure that Charlie was simply confusing the hands of the clock. He had the minute hand and the hour hand reversed. I was pretty sure that if I attempted an explanation of Charlie's error, he would become even more confused.

"Charlie, would you please take off your watch and give it to me?"

"Why?"

"I just want to check it out against mine. We seem to be having some clock issues here. Maybe I can fix it with a new battery."

"Okay." Charlie removed the watch and handed it to me.

I left the room with the watch. Within the minute, I returned with the photo album. It was one of Charlie's favorite albums. I had made it right after our return from Hawaii.

"Oh look!" Charlie said. I glanced at the page that had caught Charlie's eye. "You were just a kid then," he added.

"Those were good times, weren't they, Charlie?"

"Yeah, I gave you a flower to wear in your hair. I give you flowers every day, don't I?" Charlie asked. He

91

was back nearly three decades in time where his memory was not such a mechanism of betrayal.

I said, "Charlie, you were great at finding just the right flower." Then, I left the room and Charlie continued to make comments about the pictures he viewed. He had viewed the same album earlier in the day. And, he would view it again tomorrow, and the next day, and the next.

***

Using our ABC model, I ignored the accusation Charlie had made and stopped to notice his affect. I noticed the look of confusion on Charlie's face. His behaviors were not problematic at that time. There was cognitive confusion that required attention before anxiety set in.

Those with progressive dementia oftentimes have fixations with food and many will overeat, not realizing they have just eaten. Others will not eat unless the food is placed in front of them. Hunger signals are no longer reliable indications of a need to be nourished. And caregivers are oftentimes frustrated by repeated demands to eat.

Charlie's cognitive confusion probably stemmed from a visual distortion, confusing the hands of the clock. This is also a visceral distortion. It would have been an inane exercise to attempt to convince Charlie of the time. Time was not the issue. Confusion was the issue.

At times, we caregivers must chose a fork in the road. One road leads to a destination of attempting to solve a problem. The other road leads to producing a distraction which will simply end the issue and get on with the processes of the day.

Oftentimes, the best way to assuage a state of confusion is to remove the source of confusion and then, introduce a known element to the dementia patient. In this case, Charlie's watch was removed and the photo album was available. Charlie's immediate memory was of a personal moment of efficacy. Long ago, he had brought me flowers every day and it made him feel good. My response was a simple and logical reinforcer. I chose the fork in the road and it ended Charlie's confusion about time. My choice of that particular fork also brought moments of pleasure to a confusing situation.

If you're not making mistakes, then you're not doing anything. I'm positive that a doer makes mistakes. John Wooden

24.

Endurance

About 600 BCE, there was a man by the name of Siddhartha Gautama. He later became known as the Buddha. When I studied World Religions as a minor to my psychology classes in undergraduate school, I came across this quote which has remained a motivator for me throughout my years as a caregiver:

"Endurance is one of the most difficult disciplines, but it is to the one who endures that the final victory comes."

After thinking long and hard about the components of the concept of endurance, I believe the following attributes most accurately represent the endurance of caregivers:

E   Escape from negative emotions. If you cannot distance yourself from anger, hurt and disappointment and realize that your loved one is communicating something vital to her/his own stability, you will lose opportunities to grow as a caregiver.

N   Nurturance. An underlying respect and love for yourself and your loved one as human beings is essential to being able to transform yourself into someone available and dependable.

D   Defiance. You need to be able to defy time-honored expectations of yourself and your loved ones. Authoritarian rules of what "should be" or "ought to be" have no place in caregiving. Yours is now an unpredictable world and you need to begin to learn how to stabilize what you can. You need to be able to put aside dreams of what your life would be and deal in the reality of what you have.

U Understanding. Understanding of your life as it is remains crucial to making changes which are essential to caregiving. Denial of the loved one's dysfunctional emotions, behaviors and cognitions only delays a process which can potentially become manageable.

R Restraint. As a caregiver, we must resist allowing our own emotions to become the center of attention. Instead, we hope to resist the urge to fight for our own honor and instead, get into a problem-solving mode. Once we throw emotional restraint out the door, we lose the opportunity to act effectively as caregivers.

A Ardor. Yes, ardor. Despite the need to maintain a stable emotional presence, we need to address caregiving problems with ardor, with passion and zeal. We must convince ourselves that, with practice, we are skilled in the art of problem-solution. When we get excited about an opportunity to learn about ourselves, our own feelings of inadequacy and anger are replaced with a passion to help our loved one as well as with feelings of personal efficacy.

N Novelty. For me, this is one of the more pleasurable parts of the caregiving experience. When I attempt to use my own creativity to problem-solve and the result is then a reduction of Charlie's anxiety and/or confusion, I get pleasure in being able to use my brain to help bring stability to one whose own cognitive functioning is an ongoing source of consternation.

C Constancy. Practice of restraint combined with ardor for learning bring creative problem-solution results. This results in feelings of constancy as a caregiver. It is a feeling that no matter what happens, we can act and react to whatever comes our way.

E   Empathy. We all have compassion for our loved ones. But, our own anger and frustration oftentimes prevents a sense of being able to fit inside the emotions of another and assume the sense of fear and anxiety. With practice, we are able to set aside our own immediate emotional needs and truly walk in the shoes of our loved ones as they take their journey through a foreign environment.

I cannot think of a greater journey of endurance than the one of those who become caregivers to those with progressive dementia. It is a commitment to one who truly walks a lonely and unknown path.

And the final victory….just what would that be? If is an individual experience. For me, victory is knowing I have done my best.

Accept the challenges so that you can feel the exhilaration of victory. George S. Patton

25.

Restraint Breakers

Perhaps the most difficult action in the process of positive reinforcement is the restraint breaker. No matter how much we practice, even patients in the moderately severe progressive dementia process can manage to break a caregiver's chain of composure.

Take your memory back to the simple child's game of Red Rover. All you have to do is link arms with someone who has your own arm strength and it seems as though no one can break the chain. But then, every so often, the smallest child on the opposing team has just the right technique. You and your partner momentarily drop your guard and the seemingly weaker child breaks through.

It almost seems as if dementia patients somehow retain their ability to rile the caregiver, especially when the caregiver is emotionally weakened and physically weary. These are classic chain breakers in the repertoires of most patients with progressive dementia:

"'You're mean."

"You don't care."

"You're just trying to trick me."

"You're the one with the memory problems."

"You should have told me that." (This statement generally follows several repetitions from the caregiver.)

"I don't want to." (This statement almost always follows multiple tasks already being done by the caregiver.)

"Stop yelling at me!" (This happens when the voice is raised with a hearing impaired patient. At times they are more sensitive to voice than at other times.)

Most of these seeming personal attacks against the caregiver stem from anxiety over being unable to comprehend the environment or from apprehension that the patient is no longer in the favor of the caregiver.

If we reply in a negative manner to a loved one who attempts such a restraint breaker, we have lost any opportunity for a successful outcome. Sometimes, the thinking of the dementia patient is so warped that the restraint breaker is totally unconnected to a precipitating event. There is no logical connection; therefore, any reply to such a comment is also irrational.

If we stop and look directly at the loved one, we will generally see the common emotions of fear, confusion and anxiety, we will generally be able to replace our feelings of anger and frustration with compassion. Pulling back and looking for goodness in the loved one's affect, behavior or cognition is then a successful restraint on the part of the caregiver.

However, if we see anger or threat in the face of the loved one, redirection or even leaving the scene for a brief time may be the prudent caregiver action. At times, the loved one momentarily forgets the caregiver and is surprised by his/her presence. In that instance, it may be best to simply leave and then come back and approach slowly with a smile and an even tone of voice. This allows the loved one to become reacquainted with the caregiver.

My own husband has developed an exaggerated startle response. It he does not see or hear me approach, even a kind statement can startle and disorganize him. It is the basic "fight or flight" response we learn early in life.

98

We caregivers must be sure that there is a caregiver/loved one connection before successful reinforcement can occur. Generally, even if disoriented, the dementia patient will recognize a certain tone of voice or a common comment such as a general greeting. I oftentimes "reacquaint" my husband with our relationship with such an approach.

Life is 10% what happens to you and 90% how you react to it.

Charles R. Swindoll

26.

Building Skills

In order to build skills which become reliable and automatic, let's pick apart the following scenario:

You are tired. Your loved one has watched you clean the house and now, it is dinner time and you need a rest. Instead, your loved one says:

"You forgot to do the dusting. I watched you and you didn't do it".

"Well, if you watched, why didn't you do it? You saw how hard I was working. Why do I have to do everything around here?" *You throw a dust cloth at your loved one and hope that just maybe, s/he will do something to show you some appreciation."*

"I don't want to."

"Well, I've got news for you; I don't want to do it but I have to! I have to do everything. I don't get to sit and watch like you!" *You know you are getting out of control but right now, you need to vent.*

You watch as your loved one smiles and begins to taunt you with your own actions. "You threw the cloth at me! You're angry. You shouldn't be angry all the time. Look how red your face is!"

Oh yeah, you're really angry now. Not only did your loved one do nothing to help, s/he's making fun of your frustrations. You go over and raise your voice. "I just hate this! You see me do all this work and it's for both of us! At least, you could show me a little appreciation!"

100

What you really want is for your loved one to take you in h/his arms and be the person s/he was before. At that moment, it's about the only thing that will pacify you and of course, you deserve that. But, it's not going to happen. That was then and this is now. It should stop here, but it doesn't.

Even though you remain silent, the restraint breaker has been successful. Your loved one says, "I'm hungry. What are we having for dinner?"

Dinner is the last thing on your mind. Your loved one used to be the cook and now, that's just another thing to do that you don't really want to do. You know you should stop but your exhaustion has turn to angry energy and you stay in the conversation.

"I'm not fixing dinner. If you're hungry, go get it yourself!"

Obeying your instructions, your loved one gets up and heads for the kitchen. You raise your voice again and say, "You can't use the stove! Hey, get away from there!" *And you race into the kitchen and turn your loved one around and instruct him/her to go sit down.*

Your loved one has done as you requested and for some reason, that makes you even angrier. You don't want to fix dinner and you still feel unappreciated. Your loved one has allowed you to negatively reinforce his/her behaviors and, being exhausted, you fell for it. Your loved one has broken through the restraint barrier and you're not sure you even want to play the game anymore.

***

Where did you go wrong? You didn't stop. You were too tired. You allowed normal emotions to control your behavior, as if you were talking to a rational person.

It was one of those days when you wanted magic. You wanted your loved one to be okay, even if just for a moment. There is not a one of us caregivers who don't want that. But, there are no miracles in progressive dementia and the best we can do is to protect ourselves. In the above scenario, we simply left ourselves open for additional hurt.

So, let's go back. Let's go back and do it more effectively. There is no *right* way, but there is a more effective way.

***

You have finished your work and you sit down next to your loved one as s/he says:

"You forgot to do the dusting. I watched you and you forgot to do it."

"Yeah, you're right, Charlie, I did forget to do that. It might be a chore for tomorrow. I'm just so tired tonight. Maybe you could do it tomorrow." (You have acknowledged the loved one's perceptions and stated your own feelings.)

"I don't want to."

"Let's wait to tomorrow. Let's see how we both feel tomorrow." (You have resisted the urge to have the tasks completed today and you have given a common ground to your loved one. You both feel tired.)

In this scenario, the cloth would not have been thrown and the ugly words would not have been spoken.

"I'm hungry. What are we having for dinner?"

"Hmmm, I really don't feel like working in the kitchen tonight, Charlie. I guess we could heat up last night's soup or we could order a pizza." *(You have stated a fact and given your loved one a choice. Either choice should be acceptable to you.)*

"I like a pizza. Soup is too runny. I spill it all the time."

"Pizza would taste good, Charlie. Let me clean up and I'll make the call for pizza."

In this scenario, you have stated facts and reinforced your loved one by asking her/him to make a choice for you both. This is a validating thing for a dementia patient. If you offer a choice and either is acceptable for you, you have actually empowered your love one and given her/him a moment of feeling effective. However, as the dementia progresses, many loved ones cannot make a decision at all. In that case, you will offer the desired food and state that it is a favorite for you both.

***

Let's try another one. On this day, you are just itching to get out. It's a weekend and the weekends are when you and your loved one always did special things. You think for a while and then suggest:

"Let's go out and do something, Charlie."

"What?"

"Oh, I don't know. I just feel like getting out."

"Me too. Let's go to the beach."

(Well, now this is the last thing in the world you want to do. You don't want to have to pack up everything.

You know your loved one can no longer walk the beach with you. In fact, s/he will probably be needing the restroom every five minutes.)

"No, that's too much trouble. You can't walk that well anymore and it's too hard to get to the bathroom."

"I want to go to the beach."

"We're not going to the beach! What on earth are you thinking, Charlie? You can't do the beach thing anymore. Now, forget it!"

"Well, I want to go out."

"I do too, but it's not much fun anymore."

"We can still have fun."

"How, Charlie? Just tell me how we're going to have fun when you can't do things anymore?"

"I can so."

"Charlie, be realistic. It's way too hard for you to walk. Maybe we should just forget it. I can turn on the television for you. Maybe there's a game on."

"I want to go out."

"Charlie, for Pete's sake, let it go! Don't make me hurt your feelings. I'll turn on the television.'

"I don't want the television. I want to go out. You said we could go out."

"Charlie, please let it go! Please, just let it go."

"Don't yell at me."

"I wasn't yelling. You can't hear if I don't speak up.'

"You hurt my ears."

"Oh, for gosh sakes, just let it go."

(You leave the room in disappointment. It stays with you for some time and you're not sure how you got yourself into a situation. Neither you nor your loved one got what you wanted.)

***

You had a great idea. You wanted to treat yourself and your loved one to an outing. But, you did not prepare yourself mentally. You used your old programming (your old mind-set) and the variables no longer apply. Your good intentions were thwarted before you even started. Let's try it again.

***

"Charlie, I feel like getting out for a while."

"Me too."

"So, we always love to drive to the beach. We could just take our chairs and sit toward the back of the beach. We can watch the sun set and listen to the tide coming in. It is something we both like to do,"

"Okay."

And you go to the beach. You have specified where you will go. It is senseless to give open-ended opportunities to one with progressive dementia. They simply cannot make choice selections because they cannot retain the myriad of choices. If you must allow a choice, then simply provide two choices. Again, both choices would be acceptable to you. That way, your loved one with dementia feels valued for making the choice and you already know ahead of time that you will not have to fight for what you really want to do in order to relax.

Infuse your life with action. Don't wait for it to happen. Make it happen. Make your own future. Make your own hope. Make your own love. And whatever your beliefs, honor your creator, not by passively waiting for grace to come down from upon high, but by doing what you can to make grace happen…yourself, right now, right down here on Earth.

Bradley Whitford.

27.

Receiving Feedback

There are numerous ways in which caregivers may receive feedback relative to their actions and reactions toward the loved one in their care. How the feedback is assimilated by the caregiver is critical to the emotional wellbeing of the loved one as well as the emotional stability of the caregiver.

Feedback is generally a wonderful opportunity for growth on the part of the caregiver. Sometimes, it can stop maladaptive behaviors in their tracks. If we are getting out of control emotionally and someone brings this to our attention, we need to get past the immediate emotional hurt and switch to a learning mode. This takes practice and the first step of that practice is to delay a response and listen.

For the sake of practice, we will assume that your loved one is at least in the moderate stage of his/her progressive dementia where verbal and behavioral actions are now noticeable to others. In this scenario, you have just received a phone call from the day care in which your loved one is placed. You love the day care; they are your lifeline to sanity. They allow you several hours in the day to experience "normal" social interaction if you choose to use your time in that way. You hope the day care will be available forever. And then, you pick up the phone and your bubble bursts.

"Hello."

"Hi Karen. This is Bev from the Sunset Center."

You immediately recognize the voice of the Director of the day care facility and you tense.

"Oh hi, Bev. Is anything wrong with Charlie?"

"No, don't be alarmed. I just want to bring a couple of things to your attention.

But, already, you **are** alarmed as you reply, *"Okay."*

"Well for the past week or so, Charlie has been going to the hallway to go to the restroom. He doesn't always immediately return to the group room so we send an attendant to make sure he's alright."

So far, this isn't sounding too serious, so you relax just a bit as you reply, *"What are you telling me?"* But then, you begin to anticipate what is coming and your defensive mode kicks in.

"Ummm..." the director replies. Then she continues. *"Well, it seems that Charlie is wandering here. He goes into staff offices and begins to look at personal things. That's not an acceptable behavior."*

That's a red flag and you begin to stiffen. "Unacceptable behavior" is grounds for dismissal from the group. You begin to panic and you blurt out, *"But I thought that's why Charlie was in the group....so you could watch out after him."*

"Sure, of course, and we do that. But, it may not be enough."

Without waiting for further word, you become defensive and you tell the Director that you put Charlie in the program because of his behaviors and you expect that staff is qualified to handle the situations that arise while Charlie is in the care of the Sunset Center. You hardly give the Director an opportunity to help resolve the situation and you ask," *So what else is Charlie doing that's so bad?"*

Fortunately, experience wins out as the Director calmly replies, *"Karen, I called because I want to tell you that whenever Charlie goes into the hallway to use the restroom, he will now be accompanied by one of the workers. We need to be sure he doesn't wander outside as well as assure that our staff also experience a secure environment."*

You are so relieved you want to give the director a hug and you realize how emotionally fragile you are. You pause, take a deep breath and the, you simply reply, *"Thank you, Bev. And I really am sorry that Charlie is giving you cause for concern."*

"He's really a sweet guy, Karen. But you know, the disease does continue to get worse and we need to anticipate his needs."

Now you feel a bit of a heel but you begin to listen. In fact, you've become attentive and you have switched to the learning mode. *"You said there were a couple of things, Bev."*

"Yeah, well, this one is a bit more complex," Bev states.

This time, you simply take in the statement and say, *"Okay."*

"Charlie is making some inappropriate statements in group. I intend to talk with him before he leaves today. If he comes home upset, please let me know."

"Should I talk with him about it?"

"Let me try to help him first, Karen. It's not in his character to act this way but nevertheless, we can't allow it in the group."

"Okay. Bev?"

"Yes?"

"He's been doing those things at home too. He wanders outside but so far, he has not gone off the property without me. Sometimes, if I don't approach him carefully, he will say things to me that aren't kind."

"Alright, thanks. So now we know it's probably not an isolated behavior and we may need to provide a bit more supervision."

"That's fine with me, Bev. I'm not comfortable leaving him alone anymore when he's with me. I used to run errands but now..."

"Yeah, I think we all know we're in another phase now."

"Thanks, Bev. I'm thankful for the heads up. I so much appreciate the way you look out after my man."

When you hang up the phone, you realize that you now have really important information. Charlie is not just acting out with you personally out of anger or frustration. He is apparently having difficulty processing his immediate environment in general. Furthermore, the day care center's Director has offered to work with you in attempting to control the new behaviors. Instead of feeling inadequate and angry that your plans for Charlie have gone awry, you now feel you have a partnership and you need not go it alone.

In another feedback situation, a neighbor approaches you and comments that he heard you yelling at Charlie the other day. He asks if you are okay. You could get defensive and give him a piece of your mind about minding his own business. You could deny your own actions, not wanting to look bad in front of the neighbor or risk having that neighbor report to others that you are being rough with your own husband. Those are natural responses but they are not responses that will give you an opportunity to grow as a caregiver. And so, you take your deep breath, delay a response for just a few seconds and then, you respond.

"Jim, yes you got it right. Charlie was out sweeping up the deck in the back. But, you know, lately, he just doesn't seem to have much awareness of his surroundings. He was dangerously close to the edge of the steps, so I ran out and yelled at him. I really thought he was going to take a tumble.

"Wow, so I guess you're having to really keep an eye on him, Karen."

"Yeah, it kind of a 24/7 thing now, Jim."

"I noticed the way he's all hunched over now. And he shuffles when he walks. Maybe he should use a walker."

"I have one but he won't use it. I think for Charlie, it's some kind of pride thing."

"It must be so hard to watch him fail like that. I'm not even sure he knows my name now. He smiles but gives me a blank look as if he's trying to figure out who I am."

"Yeah, he's definitely progressing in the disease."

"It's pretty hard on you."

"Yean, it's pretty hard."

"Well if I see him in danger, can I yell at him too?"

"Please do, Jim. And Jim?"

"Uh-huh?"

"I really appreciate your kindness.

There is probably not one of us who has not wondered what the neighbors think. We could just say we don't care, but the truth is, we do care. And when a neighbor notices us struggling in any manner, we need to respectfully educate. The one who educates may just be the grateful recipient of a hot dish from a neighbor some night when we, the caregivers, are simply too exhausted to prepare another meal.

Let's say that you (John) are going to meet your friend Harry for brunch today. Your wife is in the hands of a paid professional companion and you decide to treat yourself to a day out. Everything goes just fine, the handshake, the hug and the casual conversation. Harry has made superficial conversation but he then asks about your wife Mary. You figure that since he's your friend, you can speak frankly to him, and you do. At one point, Harry stops you and says:

'It sounds as things are tough for you, John. But really, isn't it a privilege to take care of Mary? After all, look at everything she's done for you all these years."

You are taken aback because you needed support and understanding from someone you trusted to provide it for you. You want to tell Harry that, no, it's not a privilege; it's dammed hard work! And furthermore, you want to tell him you haven't been sitting on your butt all those years with Mary; you have been giving in return.

Harry means well but he's probably one of those friends who has no comprehension of the day-to-day stress (and oftentimes drudgery) of the progressive dementia caregiver. You need to decide if this is the time and the place to educate him. You decide it is not.

Primarily, such insensitivity in a good friend suggests that the total lack of comprehension of your situation means he would simply not respond well to the feedback you want to give. Furthermore, he may simply be engaging in wishful thinking. Many people who like to offer their own value system to someone struggling with a difficult situation want to try to convince themselves that, in the same situation, they could act in a moral and respectful manner. And so, John simply says:

"It's not really like that, Harry." John is disappointed. It is an awkward moment to be sure, but one that can be handled with deflection. *"Are you up for dessert today?"* John asks. Harry is confused but also relieved that his friendship with John may live to grow another day.

***

In a perfect world, a caregiver will always be able to anticipate questions, well-meaning advice and ignorance from others. But none of us lives in such a world. However, if we caregivers begin to practice delaying our responses to the loved ones in our care as well as with friends, relatives and other interested parties, we have a greater sense of control. And, that greater sense of control will, in the long haul, give us caregivers a better sense of emotional well-being.

Always do your best. What you plant now, you will harvest later. Og Mandino

28.

Holding Tight and Running with It

There are times when caregivers would best remain silent and unresponsive. Take a deep breath and do not respond until you figure out if it's a time to educate or not. Here's a list of some of the common statements for which there is no hope of getting any kind of resolution:

From your loved one:

You're mean.

You don't care about me.

You never told me that.

Stop shouting at me.

You need to quit mumbling.

You don't remember anything.

You're just stupid.

I don't want to do it.

You hid it from me.

You stole it.

I don't want to.

You don't care about me.

I can do that myself.

Quit treating me like a baby.

What?

What?

What?

What?

What?

When are we going to_____?

When are we going to _____?

(Same thing – fifty more times)

From Friends, Family, Neighbors

You should feel privileged to care for

_____.

Well, you've giving back now for all those years _____did for you.

You look terrible.

You should hire some help.

You should get help.

You should take care of yourself.

You shouldn't treat him/her that way.

Well, you did make promises to her/him, you know.

Stop exaggerating.

You're just too sensitive.

Here's what I'd do.

Have you tried_____?

Ah, it can't really be all that bad.

I'd put him/her in a home if it was me.

Don't hesitate to call if you need anything at all.

List of Difficult statements to Take off and Run With

None

By now, we all understand that if something strikes a caregiver as somewhat "off," it is not the time to defend yourself or to get defensive. Even when we are tired, angry, frustrated or just plain worn out, we need to preserve our own dignity by not giving credence to words that will only make our strong emotions more difficult to handle.

There is one statement about being willing to help that deserves an answer but is probably not one you want to pick off the top of your head. It's best to reply, "Oh, I'd love that. Let me think about it."

The primary thing to remember with a loved one is that as the disease progresses, you are not speaking to a rational being. A quick response will oftentimes exacerbate a situation that might have died within minutes due to lack of memory on the part of your loved one. If you try to force a situation with someone unprepared to hold a discussion, you will never get a resolution and you will lose an opportunity to reinforce the trust you have with your loved one. Even though the conversation is lost, the feelings of chastisement, inadequacy, fear and frustration will be ongoing companions to your loved one.

The critical component of handling "off" statements with friends, neighbors and family is that outside of you and the loved one for whom you provide care, no one can be expected to know how you feel. It is that way with nearly every catastrophic occurrence in one's life. The experience is so aberrant to common experience that only the one with direct knowledge can even attempt to imagine. Accept consolation. Accept empathic statements of concern. Accept support where you can get it. But do not take off running when there is a forked path ahead. When you feel overwhelmed and it seems like the only choice is to run. Then run to your support group. They know what you need.

Your Group may be an organized group of caregivers who meet regularly (minimum of once a week), sharing the good, the bad and the ugly without fear of recrimination of negative evaluation. Your Group must be those who are in the same warrior group as you – those who understand how dramatically their life plans have been altered. Your Group needs to understand that their collective journey is not done yet.

It is not highly likely that your Group will be found among your existing friends. As close as friends may be, they are also so relieved that your battle is your battle – and not their battle. Your Group will probably start out as strangers and end up as supporters, companions and friends. They will be caregivers who are not ashamed to bare their souls and allow you to see the ugly side we all want to hide. They will be among the most courageous people you will ever want to know for they will stay the course. When the time comes that your individual group members must relinquish or share the caregiving role with others, they remain advocates for their loved ones and they will continue to help you on the completion of your own journey.

Your Group will tell you that when your loved ones must be placed, you have already met and exceeded the promises you made to siblings, husbands, wives and parents. You made those promises at a certain place and time and the spirit of your promise will continue to the end. But, those places and times when the promises were made are long past and the Group will tell you that your priority is now to save yourself. And, the Group will be with you to help you to the life that is yet to come.

You are never too old to set another goal or to dream a new dream.   C. S. Lewis

29.

Deservingness and Guilt

Deservingness is the value, worth or merit of a thing. It is by definition a highly subjective word but nevertheless, a word with which a lot of caregivers struggle.

Almost daily, situations arise in which we put aside our needs. We banish our wishes to the furthest recesses of our minds. And wants, well, we really cannot afford to dwell in the Kingdom of Want.

One of the most difficult concepts for caregivers is the idea of being deserving of a meaningful life apart from the loved one for whom we care daily. It is particularly true if you are a caregiver for a spouse, as for years and years, you have done things as a couple. You have taken meals together; you have vacationed together and you have planned a future together. Most likely that future was filled with days of travel, exploration and quality time with children and grandchildren. But now, the parameters have changed. Your spouse is no longer able to sit through a movie or eat in a restaurant without your presence causing a scene or without your being constantly on guard for something that will make others uncomfortable.

Even though you have not changed your wants, your needs and your hopes and dreams, it almost seems as though you are not deserving to go on with your life at the same time your loved one struggles to make sense of an increasingly confusing environment. Yours is such a vital and serious role that having "fun" seems to be such a discordant element in your daily life.

We caregivers used to think we were good, kind and gentle people who were deserving of good things coming our way. And, we are. But lately, we find ourselves agitated, irritated and frustrated. We raise our voices and we have negative thoughts about those we love. So, how can we reconcile those negative thoughts and emotions with being a good individual, deserving of love and kindness?

We can only feel deserving if we put aside feelings of guilt. Guilt is a feeling of remorse for some grievance. It is a feeling of pain that you have somehow wronged someone. It is a productive emotion if, indeed, you have truly wronged another living being. But, caregivers oftentimes have feelings of being imprisoned in guilt even though they have committed no grievance. The guilt tends to stem from three sources:

1) Pre-disease guilt: We feel guilty that we "should" somehow have known that our loved one was failing and we "should" have taken steps to make their lives better or more meaningful.

2) Current guilt: We feel guilt over our own feelings of being trapped and resentful that the disease has taken over our lives and that our own hopes and dreams have been placed on the back burner of life.

3) Future guilt: We have periodic thoughts of wanting it all to end, of just wishing the disease process was over. The guilt comes from wishing for the end during the living years.

Pre-disease guilt is a spurious guilt, a false sense of guilt. It is false because the nature of your loved one's disease (progressive dementia) dictates that you could not possibly have anticipated doing anything to prevent the sense of pain, loss or fear that your loved one may experience in the future. Pre-disease guilt can be self-serving in that it provides fodder for your own increased feelings of loneliness and desperation at a time when those feelings are justified and genuine. This guilt is akin to telling yourself you should have anticipated that a natural phenomenon (such as a tornado) would develop and you should have had a ready solution to prevent the disaster that was yet to come. It simply cannot be done.

Current guilt is a genuine feeling produced by the circumstances in which you now live. You feel guilty that your life can (theoretically) proceed as your loved one becomes stuck in the quagmire of a confusing and scary world. You resent the fact that this disaster is something that involves you and you oftentimes feel trapped and lonely. You have further episodes of guilt as you do things independent of your loved one. And then, you feel guilty that you now need help in the form of respite care and possibly, placement. Finally, some of us manage to conquer our current feelings of guilt and then, we begin to feel guilt over not feeling guilty!

Current guilt is something we can get our hands on and attempt to fight with all the energy not devoted to our care cuties. We must put the factual argument before ourselves at every instant when guilt appears: *Guilt is for those who truly violate the rights and boundaries of others.* As caregivers, we "give care." We do not violate our loved ones; rather, we assist them in hopes they can maintain maximum functionality. And that is a gift, not a violation.

Future guilt is a bit like pre-disease in that it simply has no basis in logical reasoning. Just as you could not anticipate that your loved one would live a compromised life, you cannot **not** have thoughts of wanting the agonizing process to reach a conclusion. It is part of the human condition to empathize with others and to wish them not to suffer. It is not that you are wishing the death of a loved one. Rather, you are wishing for the pain and the agony to end. Like pre-disease guilt, future guilt is totally out of your control and you are inadvertently adding to your own burden by taking on this kind of guilt.

As serious as your life has become, it is still yours to plan, to execute and to enjoy. It will take some effort but the effort must now be directed toward transitioning your life from "serious and purposeful" to "fulfilling and meaningful." It is difficult to do that if you use your energy toward feeling guilty.

We caregivers need to tackle guilt feelings early on, and with a sense of purpose. There is no argument **for** guilt and every argument **against** guilt in your daily caregiving routines. Use your behaviors as a guide to keeping guilt in its place. If you yell, stop in your tracks and pause, just as you would if you were going to respond to a loved one who has made an inappropriate remark. Then, apologize and assure your loved one that he/she is, indeed, loved. Look into yourself for the emotion you feel. Then, note your behaviors of the day, the various tasks you have completed for your loved one. Remember the respect you have offered to someone who is cognitively challenged. Remember the planning and execution you do each and every day, simply to keep your loved one functioning with some measure of respect. If you spend time remembering what you actually **do** during the day, there is no energy left for feelings of guilt.

If this practice sounds a lot like what you are doing in your reactions to your loved one, you are correct. You must stop your negative behavior, look into yourself for your own immediate feeling and then listen to the messages you give to yourself. They are messages of anger and personal inadequacy and frustration. They are genuine and they are natural. They need **not** be denied. But, they **do** need to be addressed.

A reaction is simply that. What you do with the reaction dictates your sense of deservingness to get on with your life. If you have truly violated your loved one rather than simply reacted to a frustrating situation, then opportunities for redemption will be readily available – probably within the next hour following the incident. Because, with progressive dementia patients, the opportunities to look for goodness in the loved one and in yourself are ongoing.

If we caregivers become stuck in the idea that a momentary reaction dictates our worth, the cycle builds. It gains a foothold in our emotional center and it runs at full speed. It must not go unattended. If you address a negative reaction and turn it to kindness and respect for your loved one, there is no need for guilt. Indeed, you may just be surprised to see your own sense of adequacy begin to build as you develop a repertoire of responses that can be used in times of fear and frustration.

30.

Finding Joy Where it Hides

For we caregivers, moments of joy are few and far between. We fight depression, anxiety and angst. We fight for some semblance of a life we believe may be lost to us. We are almost afraid to have fun again for fun is something in the past, something we believe is no longer available to us. But, it **is** there, if only we can find it where it hides.

It was Halloween and I was not in a mood to hand out candy to the dozens of children who came to our house each year for the past twenty years. Last year at Halloween, I had just had a total knee replacement and neither Charlie nor I was able to get to the door to hand out treats to precious children with looks of anticipation on their faces. This year, I would take Charlie to the mall so that we could enjoy the costumes of the children without having to pop up and down from our chairs at home.

As soon as we got to the mall, Charlie needed to locate a restroom. If fact, he required a restroom about every ten minutes at this stage in his disease. In the mall, available restrooms were not an issue as each wing of the mall had public restrooms readily available. After a very slow walk from the car to the main wing of the mall, we sat in the food court, directly across from the restroom. While Charlie took another potty break, I got sandwiches for us and returned to the seat closest to the restroom. When Charlie emerged, I waved to him and he came and seated himself.

Children and their parents began to arrive at the mall. Charlie stared in fascination and he asked why everyone was "dressed up." I explained that it was Halloween. Charlie had forgotten the concept of the special night so I explained that Halloween was traditionally the one night a year when the living and the dead could theoretically communicate with one another. Charlie was awed by the various costumes, particularly those of the children. He didn't talk about what he saw, but his usually bland facial expression had yielded to the joy of the occasion.

We finished our dinners and I marveled that I only had to do the Heimlich one time with my husband when he began to choke. It was so routine with us that my actions went totally unnoticed by the excited crowd gathering at the mall. At one point, a small child about four years of age came through the aisle, right by where Charlie and I were sitting. The child stopped and stared at Charlie. He smiled at the little girl and then said, "You are a very pretty princess." The child smiled and then, ran toward the protection of her father.

Charlie looked at me with a sense of true wonder in his eyes. He said, "It's true. It's really true!"

"What's true, Charlie?" I asked.

"You really can talk to the dead!"

That really took me aback and I guess Charlie saw the confusion on my face.

"That little girl talked to me," Charlie said. "She really talked to me!"

It then dawned on me that in Charlie's world, those with costumes were the dead and the non-costumed were the living.

It was such a delightful extrapolation that I decided to run with it. Charlie was being spontaneous and that in and of itself was a joy for me. My heart began to race and I felt a sense of joy for the first time in months. I decided to have some fun. The fun would not be at Charlie's expense. Rather, I would jump into his magical world and begin to participate.

We left the food court and Charlie engaged in rubber-necking as we slowly proceeded down the main mall courtyard. I held his hand so he would not get lost among the thousands who had come to the mall for treats.

Charlie saw a costumed women in a store, checking out a costumer and asked if I thought she was dead too.

"I don't know, Charlie. Do you think the dead know how to operate the new electronic cash registers?"

Charlie wasn't sure about that but he quickly pointed out an older man in a pirate costume talking with a younger boy without a costume. "See, he's talking with him. That proves it."

I knew what Charlie meant. He was affirming his magical belief system and he was excited with his interpretation of his world. The older gentleman looked to be the grandparent of the young boy. In Charlie's world, the older man was costumed and thus, was deceased. The boy was not in costume and therefore, he was among the living. The two were indeed communicating.

I smiled at Charlie and he added, "Besides, that guy is old and the little boy is young." My husband had offered another insight. In Charlie's world, the old would die before the young. What a wonderful thought. Charlie had an inner world that was somewhat rule bound after all. For years, I had thought that our lives were ruled by chaos theory and now, I knew that in Charlie's disordered mind,

126

there were rules that governed his thinking. What a gift my husband gave to me that night. He gave me an extremely rare glimpse into the world of the Alzheimer's patient.

We stopped in the mall corridor several times while Charlie revealed his newly-acquired concept of the living and the dead being able to communicate. For me, it was a time of joy, a precious time that we shared together. We were people-watching, just like in the "old times." All I had to do was to enter Charlie's world for a brief time and I found joy.

Prior to Charlie's illness, we had oftentimes sat on benches in the mall or outside in the park. We speculated on people's occupations and from where they might originate. Our perceptions were based upon manner of speech and sometimes, by personal characteristics. Now, Charlie was applying that concept in his magical world. His sole criteria was dress. If you looked different because you were in costume, you were not of this world.

As we entered our car that evening, I strapped Charlie in as usual. He smiled at me and then said, "I will wear a costume when I die."

I didn't have to respond to that one. I instantly understood that if Charlie preceded me in death, he intended to continue to talk with me through eternity.

It does not matter how slowly you go as long as you do not stop. Confucius

31.

Putting it All Together

You've read the chapters. My hope is that it makes sense to you. You might initially conclude that it's just too hard to execute. Wrong. It is much more difficult <u>not</u> to put the plan into action and to continue to build up feelings of frustration, anger and guilt. The effort you put into changing your reactions now is energy you can put into transitioning to a more positive life tomorrow.

The principles are not difficult:

1) Opportunities for positive reinforcement in your loved one are available affectively, behaviorally and cognitively.
2) Opportunities to catch yourself in negative and destructive feelings, behaviors and thoughts coincide with opportunities to reinforce.

The simplest interaction with a loved one gives the caregiver an opportunity to build the bond of trust and safety. The same interaction may also provide the caregiver with an opportunity to build a positive feeling of efficacy through the toughest of times.

***

I want to leave you with a simple and true story. When I was a young child, I lived with various relatives following the death of my mother. One of those caregivers was my grandfather H.D. He was a wise and compassionate man who craved the simple things in life.

H.D. taught me how to fish. He told me that if I was going to fish, I needed the entire experience. That experience included less-pleasant things such as baiting the hook and, if a fish was caught, I was required to decide whether or not to keep and clean the fish for my grandmother to cook.

I loved my days fishing with my grandfather. He talked to me as an equal and I craved the time I had with him. He taught me about the famous philosophers and how one's perspective of the world was highly subjective, depending upon personal beliefs and points of view and lifetime experience. Never was that learning as important as the day in which I cleaned my catch and discovered a sack of eggs.

When my grandfather told me that the eggs were the potential for new fish, I panicked. I was young and did not want such a grave decision to be mine. I sat on H.D.'s lap and began to cry. I was asked why I was crying and I told my grandfather that if fishing carried such important decisions, I no longer wanted to fish.

My grandfather held me and then asked me what fishing really was to me. I responded that it was helping my grandmother to pack the lunch and getting the equipment all organized. It was riding in my grandfather's Model T and bumping all over the country roads. It was learning about the thoughts and beliefs of people like Rene Descartes, David Hume, Confucius and John Locke and it was about laughing with my grandfather and eating my grandmother's homemade lunch.

H.D. listened carefully and then commented that he did not understand why I could no longer fish. He said that if fishing was all of the things I had named, I could still do that when I went fishing.

I pleaded to him that I didn't want to decide whether the fish should live or die. H.D. said he understood that feeling in someone as young as I. "But," the wise old man said, "Why can't we go fishing and you just throw the fish back in the water?"

***

And, that is the message of this book. When the parameters change and you and your loved one no longer understand how to be together with one another, you as the rational caregiver need to learn to fish in a different way. You must stop the bothersome thoughts, feelings and behaviors and learn a new way to conceptualize your experience. You can throw the fish back into the water and then, continue to fish, with all the rewards and all the frustrations that go with the experience.

If you have the courage to feel your pain and release it, your own perceived failures signal the commencement of new learning.   *Karen Pirnot*

References

Buchanan, Jeffrey and Fisher, Jane (2002)." Functional Assessment and Noncontingent Reinforcement in the Treatment of Disruptive Vocalization in Elderly Dementia Patients." Journal of Applied Behavior Analysis 1. 22-103

Heard, Kenneth and Watson, T. Stuart (1999). "Reducing Wandering by Persons with Dementia Using Differential Reinforcement." Journal of Applied Behavior Analysis 3. 381-384.

Skinner, B. F. (1953) Science and Human Behavior, Macmillan

Watson, J.D. and Rayner Watson, Rosalie (1921) "Conditioned Emotional Reactions." Journal of Experimental Psychology 3. 1-14

Glossary of Terms

Aversive Stimuli-Anything which is perceived by the dementia patient as disapproval of a thought, an emotion or a behavior. This is sometimes referred to as punishment. With dementia patients, the negative look or verbal response of a caregiver can be perceived by the patient as punitive.

Behavior Modification-This refers to changing a negative behavior into a positive behavior. With dementia patients, we strive to promote positive emotions while ignoring negative behaviors.

Extinction-The cessation of a dementia patient behavior which, from the viewpoint of the caregiver, is perceived as negative. Positive behaviors may also be extinguished if the dementia patient sees the caregiver as negative or punitive. The patient's motivation to trust and to keep trying to please the caregiver then ceases.

Perception Check-Looking for clues (affect, behavioral, cognitive) to see if the caregiver interaction has the intended effect (positive emotions) with the dementia patient.

Positive Reinforcement-This is a verbal or behavioral "reward" for the dementia patient that is perceived as positive. It may be a smile or a good word about an action performed by the patient. Even though the patient may forget the words spoken, the good feeling will carry over, creating a feeling of trust and security with the caregiver.

Premack Principle-An idea put forth by Psychologist David Premack in which a preferred reinforcer is likely to be more effective in changing negative behaviors to positive behaviors, particularly if the target behavior is one which the patient does not particularly enjoy. This could be something as simple as the patient's refusal to shower. If there is trust between a dementia patient and the caregiver, verbal approval or a simple behavior such as a hug or a touch on the arm may act as a strong reinforcer to attempt the desired behavior.

Punishment-Anything which is perceived by the dementia patient as punitive. Since the cognitive world of the dementia patient is sometimes warped, it is important to try to ascertain the emotion that the patient is experiencing in the interaction. Sometimes positive caregiver actions can be perceived by the patient as negative. Therefore, the caregiver must do ongoing perception checks.

Reinforcement-A response from a caregiver that makes it more likely that a certain behavior will occur in the dementia patient. In dementia patients, a positive response will encourage positive feelings while a negative response may cause the patient to become discouraged or suspicious of the caregiver.

Reinforcement Learning-This is the goal of the caregiver. When positive reinforcement results in the desired behavioral change (feelings of trust and security with the caregiver), we say that reinforcement learning has occurred.

Schedulers of Reinforcement-A schedule (how often the caregiver provides reinforcement) may be intermittent (every so often) or continuous (every time a positive behavior is elicited. With dementia patients, it is advised that reinforcement be delivered on a continuous schedule as the memory will not retain the previous attempt.

Shaping-This refers to reinforcing a thought, emotion or behavior that is similar to that desired by the caregiver. Dementia patients do not always have the ability to complete a task. Therefore, any attempt at helping to achieve a desired goal may be reinforced. The idea is that the patient's emotions will be positive and that emotion may carry over to the next request. Partial success is important to recognize in the dementia patient. It increases the probability that the patient may try just a bit harder the next time.

Validation-Validation of another shows respect for the person's feelings and thoughts even if the caregiver does not agree with those thoughts and feelings. It is a form of empathic concern in which the caregiver attempts to trade places and imagine the experience of the dementia patient's confusion and disorientation.

Other Books by Dr. Pirnot

GENERAL

As I Am

Just a Common Lady

The Learners of Owamboland

Keeper of the Lullabies

Traveling with Grandma

A Christmas of Grace

Eating Through the Earth

Nothing Left to Burn

CHILDREN'S PICTURE BOOKS

The Blue Penguin

A Colorful Day

Rainbows are the Best

Sam's Perfect Plan

The Door in the Floor

Night Traveler

Just Hanging Out

The Colors of Myself

Please Be My Hands

MID-GRADE READERS

Ordinary Kids Series:

Peter, the Pole and the Knob

The Above All Others Principle

Potsie and the Apparition of Brave Wolf

Morgan and Clive

The Days and Nights of Crighton Immanuel

Skymasters Series:

Galaxy Girl

Under the Universe

Through a Black Hole

The Multiverse

Silky and Sly:

The Ghost of Gasparilla

The Victorian House

To contact Dr. Pirnot **go to:**

www.drpirnotbooks.com

About the Author

Dr. Karen Hutchins Pirnot is a licensed Clinical Psychologist who has treated children and their families for decades. While in private practice in Iowa, she worked extensively with the Department of Human Services and the Juvenile Justice System.

After her move to Florida, Dr. Pirnot worked in private private practice and contracted to long term care facilities to assess and treat various forms of dementia.

Many of Dr. Pirnot's book characters are patterned after traits of the children treated in her practice. She stresses instilling a sense of efficacy in children. Adult characters are viewed as resourceful and capable of making life-changing decisions. In the course of becoming an Alzheimer's caregiver, Dr. Pirnot utilized many of the same interventions that help children toward a better quality of life. The author currently resides in Sarasota, Florida with her adult children and her grandchildren.